WHISKEY
COCKTAILS

WHISKEY
COCKTAILS

Rediscovered Classics and Contemporary Craft Drinks
Using the World's Most Popular Spirit

WARREN BOBROW

*To Fred Young, who has always
encouraged me to follow my
dreams wherever they take me.*

Brimming with creative inspiration, how-to projects, and useful
information to enrich your everyday life, Quarto Knows is a favorite
destination for those pursuing their interests and passions. Visit our
site and dig deeper with our books into your area of interest:
Quarto Creates, Quarto Cooks, Quarto Homes, Quarto Lives,
Quarto Drives, Quarto Explores, Quarto Gifts, or Quarto Kids.

Inspiring | Educating | Creating | Entertaining

© 2014 Fair Winds Press
Text © 2014 Warren Bobrow

This edition published in 2017 by
CRESTLINE
an imprint of The Quarto Group
142 West 36th Street 4th Floor
New York, NY 10018 USA
www.QuartoKnows.com

10 9 8 7 6 5 4 3 2 1

ISBN-13: 978-0-7858-3526-4

Cover and book design by Jason Tselentis
Photography by Glen Scott Photography: except pages 18 (Natallya Hora/Shutterstock.
com), 24 courtesy of the author, 46, and 128 (both Shutterstock.com).
Photo Styling by Jen Beauchesne

Printed and bound in China

Foreword

"Too much of anything is bad, but too much good whiskey is barely enough."
—Mark Twain

There's something inherently masculine about a glass of whiskey. Nothing compares to the feeling of a cut crystal old-fashioned glass in your hand. Whiskey is a drink that says "I'm the master (or mistress) of my universe." The liquid amber is like testosterone itself—potent, sexy, powerful.

During Prohibition in the United States, all alcohol sales were banned and whiskey went underground. The enterprising took to distilling at night when darkness hid the smoke from the stills creating the whiskey we know as moonshine. Whiskey could also be prescribed as a medicinal by a physician and sold through licensed pharmacies.

Modern times have made whiskey much more readily available. This means we can put the services of Warren Bobrow to good use.

Warren has been crafting "fresh" cocktails for Beekman1802.com for years, and we are thrilled that he is expanding his library of books (and our cocktail vocabulary) in this potent new collection of recipes.

Brent Ridge + Josh Kilmer-Purcell
Founders, Beekman 1802

CONTENTS

Whiskey Cocktails, Then and Now

The history of whiskey is a long and venerable one,

and Ireland and Scotland are its ancestral homes. In fact, the word "whiskey" is derived from the Scots-Gaelic phrase *uisge beatha*, or "water of life." (In some cases, of course, the "water of life" has had the opposite effect: One medieval Irish annal ascribes the death of a chieftain to overindulgence in the auld *aqua vitae*.) Over hundreds of years, *uisge beatha* eventually evolved into the word *whisky*. Note the spelling: For reasons mostly lost to history, the Scottish still spell the world without the "e," while in the United States, "whiskey" retains that missing "e." Meanwhile, tipplers in Japan, India, and Canada spell the word *sans* "e," while the Irish spelling, like the American one, favors that elusive "e." So which spelling is correct?

Both, naturally. To butcher the words of the great Bard, Shakespeare (perhaps he was a whiskey drinker when he wasn't penning poems and plays?), whiskey by any other name would taste as—well, perhaps not sweet, but certainly as smooth, rich, and heady. Today, whiskey is enjoyed by imbibers the world over—not least in the United States, where it's been part of the fabric of American life since the country was young.

Back in the frontier days, whiskey was usually quickly distilled using rye—or, in rare cases, corn—and then served up to eager drinkers within a few hours of fabrication. These thirsty crowds would have consumed their precious portions of the "water of life" in makeshift, less-than-comfortable bars, and there would have been very little, if any, embellishment to whiskey drinks during these primitive days. After all, at that time, whiskey was not a drink for polite company. Whiskey was customarily served to drinkers without ice in a small two- or three-ounce "shot" glass. Cool water, or perhaps a lukewarm beer, would be served with the whiskey, but only on the side, so that the liquor would retain its powerful clout. (Whiskey, in America's early days, was not meant to be "pleasurable": it was probably a harsh drink, prone to burn the mouth and the throat, while—paradoxically—calming and warming the body.)

Hence, we have the tradition of drinking whiskey "neat" today. Most people—your dad included, I'd wager—drink whiskey straight without mixers or ice, to enjoy the spirit at its purest and most potent. Alternatively, whiskey is sometimes served with a simple mixer: The drinker might prefer it poured over a crown of crushed ice; cooled by a cube or two of ice; or with a hit of club soda. Sure, these are great ways to savor whiskey, but it's a limited repertoire. Whiskey's pleasures are diverse and delicious. And much to the surprise of the traditionalist, it's a versatile spirit that's extremely adaptable when it comes to mixology.

Even to this day, whiskey has a reputation as a "straight" drink: that is, straight out of the bottle, straight into a glass, and straight into the mouth without the benefit of mixers, and often without tasting much of anything except the alcohol's heat. After all, experimenting with whiskey cocktails is a relatively new phenomenon. Americans only began to appreciate whiskey's versatility when the country's first true mixologist, "Professor" Jerry Thomas, published his famous book of cocktail recipes, *The Bar-Tender's Guide: Or, How To Mix All Kinds of Plain and Fancy Drinks*, in 1862. A hundred and fifty-plus years later, the whiskey landscape has changed dramatically, thanks to craft spirits producers. Craft spirits are liquors that are made in small batches by small producers, and due to the high-quality ingredients they use, they've truly changed the way we view whiskey in the twenty-first century. Creative craft spirits producers pay careful attention to the aromatics and flavor of their liquors. This results in top-notch products that are often available at elite whiskey bars and other trendy watering holes (as well as your local liquor store). But this quality does come with a price: Craft spirits, which feature prominently in this book, can be quite expensive, so do choose wisely.

The up-and-coming world of whiskey mixology is far more exciting than merely adding a few drops of water into a glass and calling it a cocktail. It's a matter of creativity, intellect, and good taste—and it's right here at your fingertips. There are reams of recipes in this book for cocktails that showcase just about every variation of whiskey, whether it's bourbon; rye; whiskeys made from alternative grains such as oats and quinoa (seriously!); "white" whiskeys such as "moonshine" (the *legal* kind, that is); or Japanese, Scotch, Irish, or French iterations of the spirit. Each style of whiskey can be mixed in a unique and tasty way, adding much-needed provenance to what is one of the most famous distilled, grain-based spirits in the world.

This book presents seventy-five new and revitalized recipes for creating iconic whiskey cocktails. For instance, rye whiskey is wonderful when served in a simple hot toddy with honey and lemon, and it's also marvelous in a Maple Smoke Fizz, a twisted take on the classic New Orleans Sazerac cocktail that pairs it with bright-red Peychaud's bitters and a dash of Herbsaint Absinthe. Then there are the Old Faithfuls of the whiskey cocktail realm, which never go out of style, such as the whiskey sour, whiskey punch, and the whiskey old-fashioned. Ever had a Scotch and soda at the end of the day, or a Manhattan or Jack-and-Coke? You're sure to love these tried-and-true classics, too.

Plus, one of my favorite things about mixing whiskey is its seasonality. It's just as much at home in a frosty, iced Mint Julep served on a sultry summer's day as it is in a mug of hot tea spiked with homemade Ginger Simple Syrup as an antidote to bone-chilling winter cold. It's quite comfortable mixed with boiling water and spiced rum in a Sailor's Grog. And combining Tennessee sipping whiskey with Vietnamese-style salted, preserved lemonade, as in the Clever Lemon Fizz, is one of my favorite flavor combinations ever.

And whiskey isn't just about drinking. It's not only a natural match *with* food, it's a great addition *to* it. My recipe for Hearty Barley, Lentil , and Vegetable Stew is just the thing to warm body and soul on a rainy autumn day. If you don't blanch at the thought of whiskey for breakfast, try A Scotsman's Flourish: The ideal wake-me-up for true *bon vivants*, it sports plenty of whiskey-soaked dried fruit and an optional dash of straight Scotch that'll put hair on your chest (whether you want it there or not).

As always, be sure to enjoy the recipes in this book sensibly—they taste better that way. I know you'll enjoy experimenting with these recipes as much as I've loved creating them, and like me, you'll be delighted and inspired by whiskey's sheer scope and flexibility.

Cheers!

Warren Bobrow

Note to the reader:

"Scotch" refers to Scotch whisky (spelled intentionally without the famous "e"), "bourbon" means bourbon whiskey, and "rye" refers to rye whiskey. By "alternative grains," I mean any grains apart from corn, rye, or wheat. "Tennessee sipping whiskey" refers to corn whiskey distilled in Tennessee, which is traditionally enjoyed at a leisurely pace, or "sipped."

Whiskey's Intoxicating History

The history of whiskey is a long and venerable one,

Whiskey is fiery, soothing, and stimulating all at once. (One writer even described it as "a torchlight procession marching down your throat.") It's been treasured as a valuable curative—but it's also been seen as physically and morally toxic: During Prohibition, the nationwide American ban on the production and consumption of alcoholic beverages that was in place between 1920 and 1933, it was *verboten,* along with all beer, wine, and liquor. But what is whiskey, anyway?

Simply put, whiskey is a distilled beverage made from a mixture or "mash" of one or more grains, including corn, rye, barley, and wheat. Then it's aged in wooden, usually oak, barrels before it's bottled and sold. Whiskey usually clocks in at around forty percent alcohol by volume (ABV), or eighty proof, and it's made in just about every country in which grain can be grown. The history of American whiskey is a particularly august one, since it's been around since the nation was in its infancy. Whiskey, in its earliest American incarnations, was imbibed as both a medicinal remedy and as a powerful intoxicant. It was used by early settlers in religious ceremonies. In Christian churches, whiskey was sometimes used instead of wine during communion when wine was unavailable—and it was traded to Native Americans in exchange for furs.

The early American apothecaries and snake-oil barkers who followed the tide of immigration out West had much to do with cultivating a thirst for strong drink. They created potent distilled beverages in the wilderness, including rough, mostly un-aged whiskeys, helping to develop a thirst for intoxication amongst the settlers. Early apothecary salesmen would have used "table-top distilled" whiskey in their preparations. In fact, whiskey may have been combined with the herbs and spices that were to be used as curatives— either for actual illnesses, or for those illnesses that were products of a vivid imagination. Plus, whiskey traveled well, unlike most other beverages popular at the time. While rum was the tipple of choice in many seaside cities, the raw materials for distilling it couldn't easily be transported away from the coast. Beer was too difficult to store out in the wilderness. It would have soured quickly if it couldn't be kept cool. Table wine would have turned rancid, while fortified wines such as Madeira or port would have been out of reach financially to all drinkers but the most genteel.

Whiskey was a durable product that traveled well in ceramic jugs, glass bottles, or flasks, and could be served simply in a glass without ice or mixers—a fact that cemented whiskey's position on the frontier West. With the great influx of immigration from Ireland, Scotland, Germany, and beyond, different homespun methods of distillation followed the new immigrants on their journeys across the vast continent. Whiskey was used on the frontier as medicine, for cooking, and during social gatherings, very much as it is used today.

Thus, whiskey became practically synonymous with the West of America. Even today, the very word evokes adjectives such as "tough," "rough-and-tumble," "hard-core." There's no doubt that the abundance of cheaply-made American whiskey fueled hundreds of barroom brawls as well as the popular imagination, inspiring our cinematic—and romanticized—visions of the Wild West. But the history of whiskey in the United States predates the nineteenth-century American West by nearly a hundred years. America's early years were rife with insurrections pertaining to whiskey and taxation. In 1791, rebellious settlers in Pennsylvania came to blows with the federal government in what was considered to be an act of treason. These early settlers were disgruntled by new federal taxes on the sale and distillation of spirits—and the insurrection that followed, the so-called Whiskey Rebellion, pitted small-town country folk from Pennsylvania with only limited resources against the mighty military power of the federal government. At the time, whiskey, especially rye whiskey, which was made by settlers themselves using their own surplus grain, was used in many parts of America as a form of currency. (It was even said that rye whiskey was worth more than gold.) Understandably, these settlers thought the new whiskey tax highly unfair, and even attempted to secede from the young nation. Ultimately, the federal government sent fifteen thousand armed troops to crush the fledgling rebellion, and the rebels had to submit to the new tax laws. This whiskey-fueled event marked the beginning of formalized federal taxation in America.

Some things never change. To this day, the Internal Revenue Service of the United States still oversees the production of spirits that claim the moniker "Bottled in Bond." These spirits, including some whiskeys, are distilled and bottled under government supervision. This way, the federal government guarantees the purity of the product—that is, ensuring that it's not tainted with additives or colorants—and in return, they get their tax money right up front. When a spirit is bottled in bond, it's a guarantee of authenticity, and it means, "When it comes to quality, this is the really good stuff."

Whiskey that's bottled in bond utilizes exactly the same multitude of grains as non-bonded whiskey, such as rye, barley, millet, oats, quinoa, corn, or even wheat, which are then boiled in water in a method that's not dissimilar to brewing beer. Then, important proprietary yeast strains are added to the mix, and this living slurry ferments into a liquid that is cooked under pressure in order to extract a combination of sugars and intoxicating (and highly flammable!) vapors. The heating process creates a distillate that is captured and dripped, a single drop at a time, into a vessel of either glass or stainless steel; then, the distillate is transferred to an oak barrel to age until the producer is ready to bottle and sell it. If a whiskey is bottled in bond, the bottle will boast the Federal Seal, a sign of the quality of its contents.

American Whiskeys

American whiskey is a product of the grit and guts of the men and women who forged new lives in the United States and who created a uniquely American heritage of distillation. It comes in various formats, textures, flavors, grains, and styles, and it has also been adapted to imitate different flavors and recipe styles from around the world. Some American whiskeys are reminiscent of Scotch, while others mimic Canadian whisky's slightly sweeter taste. Maple-flavored whiskies, spiced whiskies, and even new bacon-flavored whiskeys (no kidding!) are all available on today's market. That said, some of the most tried-and-true traditional varieties of American whiskey are:

Rye whiskey: In the eighteenth and nineteenth centuries, all whiskey distilled in the United States was rye whiskey. (The tastes of the era were decidedly different from our twenty-first century ones.) In terms of flavor profile, rye whiskey has a sharp, cinnamon-tinged flavor profile, and it certainly would have satisfied the tough-as-nails frontier explorers who valued the potency and alcohol level of their liquor over its flavor. With Prohibition's inception in the early part of the twentieth century, rye fell out of favor when it came to whiskey production—but today, it's regained some of its popularity. Rye whiskeys stand up to mixers well, which is why it's featured in a good chunk of the recipes in this book. Jim Beam and Knob Creek both produce rye whiskeys.

Bourbon whiskey: All bourbon is whiskey, but not all whiskey is bourbon. In order for an American whiskey to qualify as bourbon, federal law insists that it must be made in the United States and it must be made from a fermented mash of at least 51% corn. This distillate must not exceed 80% alcohol by volume. (160 proof) The distillate is cut with water and then stored in charred, new oak barrels at not more than 62.5% alcohol by volume. (125 proof) The barrels may be filled only with the bourbon one time, and then they must be repurposed. If the bourbon whiskey ages for two years or longer this product may command a higher price for the rare honor of being named straight whiskey. Four Roses, in Kentucky, Few Spirits, from Illinois, and Tuthilltown Spirits, in New York, are three examples of bourbon whiskey.

Straight bourbon whiskey: This whiskey is aged for a minimum of two years in charred oak barrels. Adding colorings or flavorings to this stuff is strictly prohibited. If you ask me, straight bourbon is *la crème de la crème* of bourbon whiskeys, since it's produced according to strict regulations, and with the very best ingredients available. Like anything else in life, you get what you pay for, and straight bourbon does carry a hefty price. But it's worth it, especially when it's produced by craft distillers, who make straight bourbon whiskey in miniscule, carefully prepared quantities; that's the way to get the best value for your hard-earned dollar. Jim Beam and Wild Turkey, for example, produce straight bourbon whiskeys.

Tennessee sipping whiskey: This stuff lives up to its name: It's whiskey that's produced in the state of Tennessee and was traditionally made to be sipped slowly. Jack Daniel's is probably the best-known producer of Tennessee sipping whiskey. Their distinctive, black-labeled bottles appear in good bars (and in private homes) all over the world, even in the smallest of villages. The Jack Daniel's proprietary method of distillation involves deep charcoal filtration: Toward the end of the production process, the whiskey is filtered through charcoal in wooden vats. This charred-wood filtration creates JD's trademark smoky flavor and balances the naturally sweet flavor of corn, its main ingredient.

It's a flavor that's unique to Tennessee whiskeys; bourbon whiskeys produced elsewhere in the United States don't possess this smokiness because they're not filtered through charcoal. If you enjoy Scotch whiskey, try a Tennessee sipping whiskey. Stylistically, they're very similar due to their smoky flavor. That said, traditional distillation laws in the state are changing, and not all Tennessee whiskey is as smoky in the nose and mouth as Jack Daniel's is (whose Black Label, in particular, is not for the faint of heart!). Craft liquor producers are now seeking new licenses that'll permit them to produce their own versions of Tennessee sipping whiskey, using the state's locally drawn, fragrant, mineral-packed water.

White Whiskey: Otherwise known as White Dog or moonshine, white whiskey is un-aged whiskey. Historically, white whiskey has had a reputation for being rough. (Or, perhaps, ruff! Get it? White Dog? Ruff? Ahem, sorry.) It's been thought of as a rough-and-ready kind of drink, likely to be served in a pail, still hot, drained off a backwoods still just a few minutes prior to consumption. And, of course, it's been rumored to be ridiculously, unbelievably, mythologically intoxicating. Indeed, true "White Dog" was practically pure ethyl alcohol, exceeding 180 proof (that's a staggering ninety percent ABV). Obviously, no liquor like the White Dog of days gone by is sold legally today. Thus, modern-day liquor producers have created new versions of the White Dog mystique: Some of them even pretty up their "moonshine" with candied fruits such as cherries or peaches, or suggest combining White Dog with soda to make it palatable. These products are not on my menu, and you won't find them in this book. That's not to say that there aren't good white whiskeys on the market—there are, and they bear no resemblance to the awful stuff called moonshine. Try Tuthilltown Spirits's Hudson New York Corn Whiskey, which is distilled from 100-percent New York corn.

Whiskey, of course, has roots in Scotland and Ireland, and today, whiskeys produced in these countries have their own distinctive production processes and flavor profiles.

Scotch whisky

Scotch whisky (note that missing "e"!) is redolent of smoke, brackish seawater, drops of tangy wildflower honey, and freshly cut herbs. Some Scotch whiskys taste like a dollop of sweet cream, while others possess the deep saline flavor of wet sea stones that've been baked for days in a peat-burning fireplace. In fact, there are countless varieties of Scotch with diverse flavors, far too many to mention here. Scotch-drinking purists often scoff at the mere idea of mixing their revered spirit with anything but a few drops of spring water. (For some, however, even *uisce* is anathema. The closest their dram will ever get to water is when it's drunk outside in the ever-present Scottish mist.) Being the Cocktail Whisperer, I beg to differ! Add a small measure of raw, locally-gathered wildflower honey, a dash of fresh lemon juice, and a spritz of

freshly drawn soda water to an ounce or two of Scotch for a sup that brings out the best in the Caledonian tipple. And that's not all: You'll find lots more cocktails showcasing Scotch in this book.

Irish whiskey

If you'll pardon my Cocktail Whisperer's take on the old saying: Where there isn't smoke, you won't taste fire. Irish whiskey is produced without the (sometimes overpowering) peat smoke flavors that give Scotch whisky, distilled just across the ocean from the Emerald Isle, its unique flavor. That's because germination of the grain, often barley, takes place using heat, not smoke. As a final step in the production process, Irish whiskey is aged for three years in wooden casks. It's sometimes sweeter against the tongue than its Scottish counterparts, but that's not to say that all Irish whiskey is sweet. Small-production craft distillers in Ireland are beginning to create new styles of whiskey, some of which are already revealing gorgeous notes of toasted grain. Bushmills and Jameson's, two of Ireland's most famous distillers, both produce good blended and single-malt whiskeys. Truly, to drink Irish whiskey is to drink this lush country's liquid history.

Japanese whisky

It doesn't sound like a terribly traditional Japanese drink, but whisky (no "e" again, in this case) is hugely popular in Japan. Today, the country's whisky distillers are practically beating the Scots at their own game—the game of distillation, that is. The Japanese are crafting super-premium, luxury whiskys that are being enjoyed all over the world. As with Scotch whisky, every sip of Japanese whisky features that unmistakable scent of peat smoke, then widens into the sweetness and long finish provided by the slowly cooked grains that lend liquid sophistication to the sup and simply shimmer across the palate. Enjoying Japanese whisky can be every bit as elegant and pricy—if not more so—as some Scottish single-malt whiskys. Plus, it doesn't have to be drunk neat: It's just marvelous with a splash of seltzer water and a teaspoon of one of Japan's other great exports, sake, swirled with green tea. It's also expressive in a head-cold-busting hot toddy that combines freshly squeezed yuzu juice, hot cider, and raw honey.

French whisky

Yes, France produces whisky, too. But whatever you do, don't mistake it for cognac. Cognac is a grape-based spirit (distilled wine, essentially) that's aged in oak barrels for at least two years. Today, a burgeoning craft distillation movement in France is using similar techniques to produce whiskey made from local grain. (The grape and the grain: together at last!) After distillation, this grain-based liquid is aged in used cognac barrels, which ensures that each sip is mouth coating, soft against the tongue, and boasts an extremely long finish—making this whisky the very embodiment of luxury. French whisky is delicious served lightly chilled with a splash of fresh grapefruit juice and club soda—it makes a great *aperitif*. And it's a marvelous *digestif*, too: Try pouring a splash into your coffee after dinner. French whisky isn't very well known on the global market at the moment, but with France's committed, creative craft producers and the excellent local ingredients available to them, this certainly won't be the case for long.

Indian whisky

Since the 1980s, India, like Japan, has been giving Scotland a run for its money when it comes to the whisky making game. And that's a bit of a surprise. Why? First of all, India is part of an equatorial climate zone, and its off-the-chart temperatures can be overwhelming to both humans and the production of distilled spirits. After all, whisky's ancestral homes are Scotland and Ireland, where early producers distilled their liquor in climates far cooler than India's—and for longer periods of time. In India (except, perhaps, in the far northern Himalayan Mountains where logistics make it impossible to distill whisky anyway), the temperature is hot for most of the year. That, coupled with the high humidity, makes the aging of whisky a far faster process than it would be in Europe. However, the final results are incredibly delicious.

Indian distillers are beginning to experiment with whiskies bottled at cask strength—a potent reminder that great whisky certainly doesn't have to come from Scotland. (A word of warning, though: Most Indian whisky is not actually made from grain. Instead, it's often distilled from sugar cane or molasses and is more of a flavored whisky substitute. The label on its bottle may hint at a fine Scottish heritage, but don't be fooled: The ingredients are anything but pedigree. I'd advise you to steer well clear of this liquor, and be sure you're buying grain-based Indian whisky when you invest in some. Rum-based "whisky" of this sort possesses all the stuffing to give you one of the most memorable hangovers of your life. Keep a large bottle of Fernet Branca handy for any such experiments into foolhardiness.)

The Cocktail Whisperer's top tips for enjoying whiskey

When you're mixing a cocktail that uses great whiskey as its base, it's important to complement it with only the very best ingredients. When I make whiskey cocktails, I use only the highest-quality, freshly crushed fruit and vegetable juices, top-notch teas and coffees, excellent (and locally sourced, if possible) aromatic bitters, homemade simple syrups, and whenever possible, I stick to hand-made seltzer water.

I never use concentrated fruit juices or corn syrup–based sodas. Why ruin a good thing? Also, I recommend making your own ice from filtered water and then hand-cutting it, in order to preserve the purity of the flavors in your drinks. Cutting ice isn't as hard as it sounds, but do take care if you attempt it: Use an ice pick and a hammer, or a chisel and a rubber mallet. (You can also up your ice's wow factor by polishing it with a wet rag that's been soaked in hot water.) If you're making a cocktail with quality spirits, why ruin it with ice that tastes like that ancient pasta with garlic that's been lurking in your freezer for months? Doesn't it make sense to use excellent ingredients and homemade ice out of respect for the spirits (and your own hard-earned cash)? To sum it up: Buy the good stuff, and make your own ice. Control freezer odors by sticking a couple boxes of baking soda in it. This technique for making your ice taste better really works.

Get ready to expand your palate! Turn the page for dozens of unique ways to savor whiskeys from around the world with your friends and family. Before you know it, you'll be as bewitched by this versatile, voluptuous spirit as I am.

Tennessee Sipping Whiskey

It's a bit of cliché, but it's true: The good things in life should be savored slowly. Think: a leisurely meal at your favorite restaurant after a long, stressful week; a sensuous, full-body massage; that beautifully wrought paragraph in the dog-eared copy of *Remains of the Day* that you return to again and again for the sheer pleasure of it; an expertly-crafted cocktail. No matter what your poison is, living in the moment and enjoying every second of it is the hallmark of the *bon vivant*. And that goes for whiskey, too.

The earliest makers of Tennessee sipping whiskey sure knew it, since they perfected a whiskey that's all about the art of relaxing. Its very name describes a style of enjoying liquor that is, sadly, nearly extinct. Tennessee sipping whiskey—or, simply, Tennessee whiskey—was conceived as a spirit that could be sipped at a leisurely pace while lounging on the porch, or whiling the afternoon away in the comfort of your local bar. Sipping whiskey was not to be rushed; it certainly wasn't meant to be knocked back as a shot, or chased with a lukewarm beer (heaven forbid!). Like the very best tequilas (and indeed the very best liquors from anywhere in the world), Tennessee whiskey was made to be savored drop by drop. Over the years, however, the tipple developed a bad reputation, until the very name of this venerable whiskey became synonymous with "sending five-dollar shots of eighty-proof whiskey straight down your gullet in a single fiery gulp." And for no good reason, either. History has been far too unkind to the gentle art of sipping when it comes to these softly aromatic, traditionally American spirits. Let's stop slandering Tennessee sipping whiskey's good name; it's time to restore it to its rightful place!

But first, what is the stuff, and what makes it so special? For all practical purposes—including the purposes of this book—Tennessee sipping whiskey is simply straight bourbon whiskey produced in the state of Tennessee. In the early nineteenth century, there were over fourteen thousand registered distillers in the state. Then, in the 1920s, Prohibition happened, making the sale of alcohol illegal. As a result, the vast majority of whiskey distillers went out of business and never resurfaced. Today, partly due to strict liquor legislation in some of the state's counties, there are still only a handful of distillers in operation (in comparison with the numbers of the early twentieth century, at least).

Whiskey aficionados need not fear, though: With new legislation in the works regarding the sale and production of liquor in many counties in Tennessee, it's likely that the growth spurt that's already visible in Tennessee whiskeys will continue and that the fledgling industry will thrive. One of the best—and most widely available—examples of Tennessee whiskey is Jack Daniel's. When it's made, the whiskey is filtered through charcoal in wooden vats, a technique that imbues the liquor with JD's unmistakably unique smoky flavor and balances the naturally sweet flavor of corn, its main ingredient.

Feel free to use Jack Daniel's for any of the recipes in this chapter. You can snag a bottle of JD for anything from $15 to $100, depending on your tastes and your budget. (Be warned, though: JD's Black Label stuff is not for amateurs—it's harsh. Their single-barrel whiskey that's been aged for twelve years, however, is as good as, if not better than, many single-malt Scotches.) Jack Daniel's is easy to find almost anywhere in the world. That said, though, there are also a number of independent, craft producers of Tennessee whiskey who are turning out top-quality spirits. See what's available in your local liquor store, or try ordering online.

Let's put the "sipping" back in Tennessee sipping whiskey! This chapter gives you plenty of reasons to embrace this highly versatile old friend of the cultured drinker. Try a Clever Lemonade Fizz, which combines easily homemade, Asian-style lemonade with whiskey, fizzy water, and a dash of sea salt for an aperitif that's truly exotic. Or, if you have company on a cold winter's day, whip up a batch of Hot Apple Pie Old-Fashioneds: Grilled fruit muddled with whiskey and apple cider are just the thing for sipping in front of the fire as a nightcap. If you're sweltering in high-level heat, you'll want something to help you chill out, so rev up the blender and make yourself a couple of the Cocktail Whisperer's seriously twisted take on the classic Bushwhacker: This version, the potent Bushwackah (and yes, that's how it's pronounced), replaces part of the rum with whiskey, which marries surprisingly well with luscious coconut crème and a scoop of coffee ice cream. Oh, and party-givers, take note: Nothing pleases guests as well as To The Disfavor of Some Gentlemen punch. Consisting of grilled citrus fruits, fresh thyme, whiskey, and sparkling water, it makes a light, subtly flavored tipple that's great with hors d'oeuvres just about any time of the year. Thirsty yet?

Note to the Reader:

All recipes make a single serving,
unless otherwise indicated.

Visionaria Cocktail

This twist on the famous Arnold Palmer cocktail is truly the stuff of dreams. It combines graciously exotic jasmine tea (don't use jasmine *green* tea, though: that's different!) with homemade ginger syrup in a tall glass—and it's the perfect showcase for Tennessee sipping whiskey. Fresh lemon juice and a hit of seltzer water give it a refreshing kick—and if you make your ice with jasmine tea, too, you can be sure your Visionaria won't get watered down over the course of sipping. Although its taste is sophisticated, there's nothing complicated about this cocktail; it's as easy to make as its ingredients are to find. The Visionaria is a great match for salty snacks, so it makes a nice aperitif. Alternatively, enjoy it on its own; it's just the thing to accompany a lazy afternoon of daydreaming.

Ice made from strongly brewed jasmine tea

2 ounces (60 ml) **Tennessee sipping whiskey**

1 ounce (30 ml) **lemon juice**

½ ounce (15 ml) **Ginger Honey Simple Syrup (see page 156)**

2 ounces (60 ml) **strongly brewed, cooled jasmine tea**

1 ounce (30 ml) **seltzer water**

Lemon pinwheels drizzled with a little Ginger Honey Simple Syrup

Add the jasmine tea ice to a tall Collins-style glass, and then add the whiskey. Top the whiskey with the lemon juice, and pour the chilled Ginger Honey Simple Syrup and cooled jasmine tea over the mixture. Finish with the seltzer water, and garnish with the syrupy lemon pinwheel. Then, just kick back and relax.

Cigar Divan on Rupert Street

Back in the day, New York City's far Upper West Side was elegance itself. This cocktail takes its name from an imaginary shop that could have made its home there, since the cigar divan itself was a symbol of moneyed leisure. Drinkers would have whiled the afternoons away in such an establishment on a low chair (or divan), cigar and cocktail in hand and the world at their feet. (Daytime drinking would be the specialty *du jour* back then. Today, of course, it's best enjoyed on special occasions only!) Anyway, you can rest assured that this cocktail is no run-of-the-mill Jack and cola. It combines Tennessee whiskey's inimitable smokiness with a dash of fresh citrus juice, handcrafted bitters, and cane-sugar cola for a tipple that's for grown-ups only. (Try not to resort to big-name colas made with corn syrup—the quality of the ingredients makes all the difference. Trust me.)

2 ounces (60 ml) **Tennessee sipping whiskey, such as Jack Daniel's**

2 ounces (60 ml) **Mexican cola (or any good handcrafted cola—ideally made with pure cane sugar)**

¼ ounce (7 ml) **each of lime and lemon juices, strained to remove pulp**

3 drops **Mexican mole bitters (or Angostura bitters)**

Hand-cut ice cubes

Drip the bitters down the inside of the glass, so as to coat it lightly. Then add the hand-cut ice cubes (the rougher the cut, the better; this'll keep the ice from diluting your drink). Add the whiskey, then the cola of your choice, and finally, pour in the juices. Stir the drink gently, and sip carefully. Cigar divans are optional.

Clever Lemonade Fizz

I'm a huge fan of Vietnamese salty lemonade, an ultra-refreshing drink that uses *chanh muối*, or lemons preserved in salt, as its base. It's not as weird as it sounds. An Asian home remedy that's as old as the hills, *chanh muối* has been credited with curing everything from head colds to nausea—and it's a surprisingly versatile and delicious creature. Don't worry about preserving lemons yourself: They're easily found in most Asian supermarkets. This simple cocktail spikes Vietnamese lemonade with Tennessee sipping whiskey, and the result is more than clever—it's enchanting. The whiskey's tangy, smoky aroma is illuminated by deep citrus flavors enrobed in salt spray. Whip up a batch for your next barbeque, or try one after dinner as a refreshing way to end a meal.

2 or 3 **ice cubes (or one tall spear of hand-cut ice)**

2 ounces (60 ml) **Tennessee sipping whiskey**

4 ounces (120 ml) **Vietnamese Fizzy Lemonade (see page 157)**

Sea salt and Easy Home-Cured Cocktail Cherries (see page 156), for garnish

Place the ice into a Collins glass, and pour whiskey over it. Top with the fizzy lemonade, then sprinkle a pinch of sea salt over the top of the drink. Garnish with a home-cured cocktail cherry (or a maraschino cherry, if you get desperate—they're not as good, though!) and a long straw. Be prepared for an encore, though—your guests are sure to ask for seconds.

To the Disfavor of Some Gentlemen Punch

If they consider themselves to be purists, some whiskey-drinking gentlemen (and women) might turn up their noses at the very idea of punch. Are you one of them? Well, if you think "frat party" when you think "punch," think again. This liquid pleasure trip is elegant, sophisticated, and subtly smoky. Grill your pineapple and citrus fruit before you juice it—the fruit becomes intensely, beguilingly sweet, and complements the smokiness that's the hallmark of Tennessee sipping whiskey. Also, I recommend saving yourself the headache the next morning and use sparkling mineral water instead of sparkling wine—you won't miss it, since the grilled fruit/whiskey combo gives this Carribeanesque punch all the lift it needs. The grilling and juicing does require a couple extra steps, but it's worth it. Take your time with this recipe, and build each layer of flavor into the punch. Your guests will thank you.

6 ounces (175 ml) **Grilled Pineapple Juice (see page 156)**

6 ounces (175 ml) **Grilled Orange Juice (see page 156)**

6 ounces (175 ml) **Grilled Grapefruit Juice (see page 156)**

6 ounces (175 ml) **Basic Simple Syrup (see page 156)**

About 16 **ice cubes made from frozen coconut water (unsweetened coconut works best)**

8 ounces (235 ml) **Tennessee sipping whiskey**

2 to 3 sprigs **fresh thyme**

1 liter bottle **sparkling natural mineral water**

Grill and juice the pineapple and citrus fruits. Add the ice to a large punch bowl, and then pour the juices and simple syrup over the ice. Pour in the whiskey and submerge the sprigs of thyme in the fruity mix. Finally, add the sparkling water, and stir gently (you don't want to lose the effervescence of the sparkling water). Let your guests ladle the punch into vintage Victorian teacups—and make sure you have enough supplies on hand to whip up another batch. Serves about four gentlepeople.

Help Me, Mr. Kentish!

The feisty young woman who narrates Robert Louis Stevenson's short story "Story of the Fair Cuban" finds herself aboard a ship in dangerous circumstances— including those of the mixological variety. At dinner with the ship's captain, a brisk, efficient officer called Mr. Kentish, "bade me sit down, and began to help me, and join in the meal," she says. "'I fill your ladyship's glass,' said he, and handed me a tumbler of neat rum. 'Sir,' cried I, 'do you expect me to drink this?'" She probably wanted Tennessee sipping whiskey instead. Curiously, it's a beguiling match for Chinese bubble tea: Its creamy texture is a beautiful foil for the whiskey's smoky flavor, and together, they create a remarkably delicate drink. Bubble tea is a combination of milk or coconut milk and slowly cooked tapioca, which has a sort of soft-to-the-tooth, gummy-bear consistency minus the tooth-injuring texture. I suggest using coconut-flavored bubble tea here, but feel free to use your own favorite flavor instead. Help yourself and a few friends to a Help Me, Mr. Kentish! It's sure to have you crying out for more.

8 ounces (235 ml) **coconut bubble tea (or your favorite flavor)**

2 ounces (60 ml) **Tennessee sipping whiskey**

A very wide-mouthed straw!

Fill a parfait glass with the bubble tea, and then add the Tennessee sipping whiskey. Stir gently, and then pop a wide-mouthed straw into the drink so that it's easy to slurp up the tapioca pearls. Slurp to your heart's content!

Hot Apple Pie Old-Fashioned

Traditionally, an Old-Fashioned involves muddling sugar and bitters in the bottom of a glass, then adding a citrus twist and blended whiskey. Minimalist, delicious, and very *Mad Men*! But my Cocktail Whisperer's take on this classic transforms it into a warming winter drink that's a lovechild of the Old-Fashioned and a hot toddy. It replaces the sugar with grilled fruit, the citrus with grilled orange, and the regular ol' whiskey with Tennessee sipping whiskey. And hot tea, steaming apple cider, and raw honey make it just the thing for kicking back by the fire. I recommend grilling both the apples and oranges, since it gives the drink a toastiness that can't be beat. The Hot Apple Pie Old-Fashioned will warm your hands—and the cockles of your heart.

½ ounce (15 ml) **absinthe**

Grilled, muddled fruit (grill orange slices and apple slices in a cast-iron pan, or over charcoal until grill marks appear on them—then chop into small pieces and muddle)

3 ounces (90 ml) **(non-alcoholic) apple cider, warmed through**

4 ounces (120 ml) **Tennessee sipping whiskey**

4 ounces (120 ml) **hot English Breakfast tea**

2 ounces (57 g) **raw honey (or to taste)**

Easy Home-Cured Cocktail Cherries (see page 156) for garnish

Pre-heat two mugs by filling them with boiling water, and then pour the water out. Wash each mug with ¼ ounce (7 ml) of absinthe, and then pour that out too (into your mouth, if you like!). Split the charred fruit between the mugs, then muddle them with the back of a bar spoon or the end of a wooden spoon. Pour the hot tea over the fruits, and then pour the whiskey over the hot tea. Top with the hot cider, add the raw honey to taste, and mix gently. Garnish with apple and orange slices, and an Easy Home-Cured Cocktail Cherry (throw out those red things in a jar: the homemade ones are so much better!). Serves two chilly drinkers.

Tennessee Lamentation

The Jack-and-ginger combination is much maligned. While it has all the stuffing for a flavor-driven experience that's redolent of spice and smoke, it's often ruined, unfortunately, by the use of super-sweet, cloying, corn syrup–based ginger ale instead of spicy, heady ginger beer. It's time to draw the Jack-and-ginger into the twenty-first century, via the olden days of ships and sails. How? Implement a spicy, homemade ginger simple syrup that's made with a dash of cayenne pepper and chunks of fresh ginger. That's when the J-and-G metamorphoses into something ethereal, sophisticated—and exceptionally perilous. This recipe replaces sugary, mass-produced ginger ale with a homemade ginger beer of sorts—a radical step that turns the Tennessee Lamentation into an all-out celebration.

2 ounces (60 ml) **Tennessee sipping whiskey**

½ ounce (15 ml) **Spicy Ginger Honey Simple Syrup (see page 157)**

2 ounces (60 ml) **fresh seltzer water**

1 dash **lemon bitters**

1 **Easy Home-Cured Cocktail Cherry (see page 156)**

Fill a cocktail shaker three-quarters full with ice. Add the Spicy Ginger Simple Syrup and the Tennessee sipping whiskey, and shake like crazy for about ten seconds. Strain the mixture over a single two-inch (5 cm) cube of ice (remember, hand-cut ice is best) in an old-fashioned glass. Top with the seltzer water, and add the dash of lemon bitters. Garnish with an Easy Home-Cured Cocktail Cherry. Makes a fabulous aperitif.

Abruzzo-Style *Caffè Corretto*

When I travel abroad, I pay close attention to what the locals are drinking. On a recent trip to Italy, I saw lots of people take small cups of *caffè corretto* at coffee bars in the mornings. And the actions of the barman who was preparing them were so simple and precise: He just pulled an espresso into a preheated ceramic cup, added about half an ounce of Jack Daniel's from a bottle he grabbed from behind the coffee bar, and served it up. There was a perfect, measured cadence to his movements: Take order, preheat cup, pull espresso, correct, serve, and drink (well, it was the customer who was doing the drinking, actually, but still). The whole process was so elegant that I just had to include it here. (By the way, while drinking brilliant *espressi* in Italy, I discovered that they're never served with a lemon zest twist. Serving a lemon zest twist alongside coffee is usually meant to conceal its poor quality, I think. Skip the twist!)

1 ounce (30 ml) **freshly pulled espresso coffee**

½ ounce (15 ml) **Tennessee sipping whiskey**

½ teaspoon **sugar, or to taste, plus a small coffee or espresso spoon for delicate stirring**

Preheat your espresso cup by filling it with boiling water, and then pour out the boiling water. Pull a single espresso into the cup (it should be no more than one ounce [30 ml]). Now, add the medicine: "Correct" it by adding the Tennessee sipping whiskey, and stir in a bit of sugar. Sip down in one gulp, look around, and have another. It's the Italian way!

The Cocktail Whisperer's Twisted Bushwackah

Down in the Caribbean islands, there are dozens of coffee- and cacao-flavored cocktails. The Bushwacker is one of them, and it usually calls for dark rum. In this kicked-up version, though, dark, aged rum (try a twelve-year-old version aged in American oak) shares the stage with Tennessee sipping whiskey. And it's a perfect marriage, helped along by a hit of freshly brewed, cooled espresso coffee and a dollop of coffee ice cream for sweetness. Go all out and make your own crushed ice from coconut water—it's worth it, since it won't dilute the tropical taste of the coconut cream. Oh, and take a hint from me: Don't drink too many of these while you're sitting out in the hot sun. They have a way of creeping up on you: One too many, and before you know it—Bushwackah!

2 ounces (60 ml) **dark, preferably twelve-year-old, rum**

2 ounces (60 ml) **Tennessee sipping whiskey**

3 ounces (90 ml) **espresso coffee, cooled**

Homemade crushed ice, made from coconut water

3 ounces (90 ml) **sweet crème of coconut**

1 small scoop **coffee ice cream**

4 drops **Mexican-style spicy bitters**

Add all the ingredients to a blender and process until smooth. Pour into a tall parfait glass, garnish with a scraping of fresh nutmeg, and serve. Try not to have more than two—if you do, don't say I didn't warn you.

Maple Smoke Fizz

And now for something completely different. See, I lived in southern Maine after college, and I have delicious memories of the scent of maple wood smoke, which seemed to infiltrate everything during the long winters. Same with sticky-sweet maple syrup: No matter what I do, I just can't forget the deep, caramelized aromatics of boiled sap. What if those woody, maply scents could be turned into a cocktail? This drink involves some minor pyrotechnics: It asks you to make your own smoke by lighting up a few splinters of maple wood, and then to "wash" a cocktail shaker with a few wisps of that enchanting fragrance. (Proceed carefully.) That, plus the mysterious qualities of both absinthe and Tennessee sipping whiskey, makes this unique take on the classic Sazerac truly captivating.

Maple Smoke Fizz

A few splinters of maple wood, placed inside an ashtray or a flameproof metal or ceramic bowl

2 ounce (60 ml) **Tennessee sipping whiskey**

½ ounce (15 ml) **Herbsaint or absinthe**

1 ounce (30 ml) **maple syrup**

Several dashes Peychaud's bitters

1 ounce (30 ml) **club soda**

Orange peel zest twist

Pre-chill your cocktail glass by filling it with ice, cold water, and the Herbsaint or absinthe. Then pour the mixture out (consider drinking it—why waste fine spirits?). Using matches or a lighter, carefully light the pieces of maple wood so that they kindle and smolder, producing smoke. Hold a Boston shaker over the miniature fire, letting the sweet wood smoke gather inside. Then, fill the Boston shaker three-quarters full with ice. Add the Tennessee sipping whiskey, then the maple syrup. To the cocktail glass, now chilled and tinged by Herbsaint or absinthe, add several dashes of Peychaud's bitters. Finally, strain the maple smoke Sazerac into the cocktail glass, top with the club soda, and garnish with the orange peel zest, twisting it slightly to release the fragrant orange oils from the skin. Sip—and start making another immediately.

General Jack's Crisp Apple Fizz

This cocktail celebrates those late September days when the sunlight becomes syrupy and mellow, shadows lengthen, the air takes on that bracing, autumnal crackle, and apple trees yield their bounty. Out here in western New Jersey, we're blessed with trees that produce gorgeous cider apples. Cider—and all things that smack of apple, really—is a great match for the smoky flavor inherent to Tennessee sipping whiskey. Here, whiskey, apple brandy, and apple cider are rounded out with a homemade honey simple syrup and doused with seltzer water just prior to serving for a drink that's the essence of fall. Plus, when you mix Tennessee sipping whiskey with apple cider, magical things happen: The world takes on a lovely golden hue, and troubles seem just a bit further away.

2 ounces (60 ml) **Tennessee sipping whiskey**

½ ounce (15 ml) **100 Proof Apple Brandy (Like Laird's)**

½ ounce (15 ml) **unfiltered apple cider**

½ ounce (15 ml) **Raw Honey Simple Syrup (see page 157)**

1 ounce (30 ml) **seltzer water**

Extra-long twist of grapefruit zest

Fill a Boston shaker three-quarters full with ice. Add the Tennessee sipping whiskey, the apple brandy, the apple cider, and the Honey Simple Syrup. Shake like crazy for about 20 seconds. Pour over hand-cut ice in a tall Collins glass. Top with the seltzer, garnish with the grapefruit zest twist, and serve.

Chapter 3

Craft Whiskey Made from Alternative Grains

Good things really do come in small packages.

Okay, so it's a bit of a cliché, but that doesn't make it any less true. Although Prohibition effectively killed off a huge number of independent distillers in the first half of the twentieth century, the whiskey landscape looks completely different in the fledgling years of the twenty-first. Today, small-producer, or "craft," distillers are popping up all over the United States. And they're not content to stick to the triumvirate of corn, wheat, and barley, the grains from which whiskey is traditionally made. Instead, these independent distillers are experimenting with alternative grains and are establishing a new set of rules for what makes great whiskey. Of course, distilling is an ancient craft and, to use another apt cliché, there's nothing new under the sun. In the past, distillers have tried to turn just about every imaginable fruit, vegetable, and grain into whiskey, with varying degrees of success. (Turnip whiskey, anyone?) Basically, distillers of days gone by would have used whatever they had at hand to make spirits—usually, local ingredients indigenous to the regions in which they lived.

Back then it was just good old-fashioned common sense. Today, that's a concept that fits perfectly with a mixological emphasis on locally sourced ingredients and *terroir*—that is, the way a dish or a beverage evokes a particular landscape. Thanks to the rising popularity of distilling with alternative, artisan grains, whiskeymakers have more raw materials to work with than ever before. (And, even more importantly, the arcane laws forbidding any kind of distilling at all have been changed in many states, so that distillers can actually get on with the job.) Sure, producers both large and small are still creating excellent spirits from the venerable whiskey-friendly grains corn, wheat, or barley. But alternative grains seem to offer craft distillers new ways to shine. This is great news for the discerning drinker, for it means that she has a whole new world of whiskeys at her fingertips, including quinoa whiskey, wheat whiskey, oat whiskey, hopped whiskey, spelt whiskey, and even millet whiskey.

Gluten- and wheat-free foods are all the rage these days: They're not just for celiacs anymore, and that means Americans are enjoying a wide variety of artisan grains both on their plates and in their cocktail glasses. Quinoa, for example, has enjoyed a huge spike in popularity. It's a good source of complete protein, and it's super-versatile (try replacing couscous with quinoa in just about any recipe—it's delicious). Indigenous to South America, it has a toasty, deeply earthy flavor when distilled. And oats aren't just for breakfast anymore: They're being transformed into whiskeys that are full of rich, creamy, caramel-vanilla flavors.

Then there's spelt: In the kitchen, it's often made into celiac-friendly baked goods, but in the distillery, it becomes a whiskey that can be redolent of yummy things like apples, warm brown sugar, or shortbread. But some craft distillers think millet makes the best whiskey of all, producing a spirit with a sweet, nutty taste. Whiskeys made from alternative grains don't come cheap, though, and you won't find many large distilleries making them because of the expense of using artisan ingredients. Therefore, most of the experimentation is done on a small scale.

Not *that* small, though. Word to the wise: Whatever you do, don't try this at home. Home craft distilling is illegal, and if you attempt it, you will absolutely risk serious personal expense in fines, and you'll almost certainly do jail time. Don't even think about engaging in any home-distilling experiments without a license from the government.

Now that we've established that you're staying out of jail, it's time to talk mixology. Whiskeys made from alternative grains are quite quaffable either neat or on the rocks, but showcasing them in carefully made cocktails is a fabulous way to enjoy them. This chapter is packed with recipes that bring out the best in artisan-grain whiskeys. Try an Oat Whiskey Mint Julep: Oat whiskey has a peppery finish that marries well with muddled mint and crushed ice. Don't wait for the Kentucky Derby—or even for summertime—to mix up a batch! Or, skip your standard Scotch 'n' soda in favor of my seriously twisted take on your dad's favorite drink. The Old Gnaw combines hopped whiskey with an easy, homemade Spicy Simple Syrup, an egg white, and a dash of club soda for a fizzy, frothy cocktail tipped with a heady spark of chile. For a decadent digestif, try my To Mr. W. E. Henley Cocktail, a tribute to the poet who cried, "I am the master of my fate: I am the captain of my soul!" It's a rich, warming mixture of spelt whiskey, hot chocolate, espresso, and orange bitters, and it's sure to stir the blood. If you feel like something fruitier, jump on the Runaway Mountain Train, which adds millet whiskey to muddled blueberries for a mojito-esque refresher that just smacks of summertime.

Read on for plenty more ways to savor whiskeys made from unusual grains. Oh, and P.S.: Like most of my cocktails, these drinks are pretty darn strong, and call for at least two ounces of spirits per serving, so I'd suggest sticking to one or two—unless you want to ride that Runaway Mountain Train straight into Hangover Central.

Note to the Reader:

All recipes make a single serving,
unless otherwise indicated.

Soft Grey Lace

This cocktail doesn't do what it says on the label. There's nothing soft or grey about it—although it is "laced" with lime and cayenne pepper for a riff on the famous (or infamous?) Moscow Mule. I like to make it with quinoa whiskey, which starts off dry on the palate, and then mellows into sweetness and a pillow-soft finish. That said, I think quinoa whiskey benefits from a fizzy mixer, hence the addition of cane-sugar beer. While the traditional Moscow Mule is little more than vodka and ginger beer served up in a mug, using quinoa whiskey and washing the pre-chilled mugs with absinthe really makes this drink shine. Plus, it's a great hangover cure: It's cold and refreshing, but the dash of cayenne will help you sweat out the effects of the night before.

2 ounces (60 ml) **quinoa whiskey**

½ ounce (15 ml) **absinthe**

2 ounces (60 ml) **cane sugar-based ginger beer**

Very light dusting of cayenne pepper

Pre-chill a mug by filling it with ice water and the absinthe, and then pour the icy mixture out (into your mouth, that is: No wasting good liquor, remember?). Pack your chilled mug with crushed ice, and then add the quinoa whiskey. Mix very gently with a long spoon. Dust the mixture with the cayenne pepper, then the ginger beer, and stir gently again. Sip cautiously, armed with cold towels for your soon-to-be sweaty brow!

Tropicalista Sunrise Cocktail

Most cocktails with the word "tropical" in their names call for rum and only rum—but if it's a recipe by the Cocktail Whisperer, anything can happen! This sumptuous drink features wheat whiskey, which is very different from whiskey made from 100-percent corn. It's softer in the mouth, and the finish goes on and on—and on. It's very elegant stuff. So treat it right: Make your own grenadine (it's not hard), and use good dark rum if you can, since it's such a match for smoky-sweet grilled pineapple juice. (The juice from grilled pineapple has a slightly "charred" taste, which rounds out the necessary acidity in this new American classic.) Go ahead and mix up a second batch, if you like—just don't hold me responsible for your headache the next morning!

3 ounces (90 ml) **Grilled Pineapple Juice (see page 156)**

½ ounce (15 ml) **Homemade Grenadine Syrup (see page 156)**

2 ounces (60 ml) **wheat whiskey**

½ ounce (15 ml) **dark rum (try twelve-year-old rum aged in bourbon oak casks, if at all possible; the deep vanilla-smoke flavors in each sip are too good to miss)**

¾ ounce (22 ml) **freshly squeezed orange juice, strained**

1 ounce (30 ml) **freshly squeezed grapefruit juice, strained**

Pinch of sea salt

2 ounces (60 ml) **club soda**

Add the first six ingredients to a mixing glass with a few chunks of ice. Stir well. Add the pinch of sea salt (don't skip the salt: It's an essential ingredient!) and stir again. Add one large cube of hand-cut ice to a rocks glass. Strain into rocks glasses, top with the club soda, and then garnish each glass with a spear of grilled pineapple and a lemon zest twist, squeezing it gently to release its fragrant oils. Serves two thirsty heads.

Cocktail Whisperer's Very Twisted Oat Whiskey Mint Julep

Over the years, I've experimented with mint juleps of all sorts. The classic version usually calls for bourbon, but I prefer the dry, peppery finish particular to oat whiskey. That said, it's not just the oat whiskey that makes this drink a bit different: The unique absinthe wash brings this time-honored cocktail into another dimension. And to make it shine, it really, truly needs fresh mint. If you aren't growing mint in your garden, or in a pot by the windowsill, you should start—you can easily grow mint indoors, even in winter. At the very least, keep a package of fresh mint in your fridge for this cocktail, in case the craving for a Twisted Oat Mint Julep strikes. I apologize to the historically minded who believe, as I did for decades, in only one recipe for mint juleps: the traditional one. But I bet this recipe will convert them.

3 ounces (90 ml) **oat whiskey**

1 teaspoon (5 g) **raw brown sugar (or demerara sugar)**

½ ounce (15 ml) **absinthe**

Crushed ice

Fresh mint (do *not* use dried mint or bad things will happen: marching armies, horses, cannon fire… don't go there! Mint bitters are acceptable in a pinch, however.)

Aromatic bitters of your choice

Bring out the freshly polished silver cup that belonged to your most favorite grand-pappy, and wash it by filling it with a mixture of cold water, ice, and absinthe, and then pour it out. Add a few tablespoons of crushed ice to the cup, a few sprigs of mint, and lightly crush the mint into the ice to release its oils and perfume. Then, add half the whiskey and half the sugar. Mix gently and thoughtfully: You're connecting with the mint julep's venerable tradition, so take care while you're doing it. Add the rest of the whiskey, then a bit more crushed ice, followed by the rest of the sugar: Mix carefully with a non-metallic stirrer until the outside of the silver cup is frosted over. Step back and admire your work, and then finish with a shake or two of aromatic bitters for an extra-savory finish.

To Mr. W. E. Henley

Named after the author of the famously rousing poem "Invictus," this is a riff on the classic, perfect-for-daytime-drinking hot chocolate toddy, and it's a first cousin of the Irish coffee. It's also an excellent vehicle for spelt whiskey, with its toasted notes of brown sugar. Served in a teacup, the W. E. Henley is classy, stimulating, and far, far too drinkable: On your tongue, it's as soft and playful as kittens cavorting on a pillow. (Or something like that.) And those orange bitters that make up the finale? They provide much-needed balance in your cup that runneth over with the sweetness of hot chocolate, simple syrup, and whipped cream. Treat yourself to one on a late Sunday afternoon, while watching *Casablanca* for the fifty-third time.

2 ounces (60 ml) **spelt whiskey**

3 ounces (90 ml) **The Best Hot Chocolate (see page 156)**

2 ounces (60 ml) **espresso coffee (made fresh or from espresso powder, in a pinch)**

½ ounce (15 ml) **Basic Simple Syrup, or to taste (see page 156)**

Homemade Whipped Cream (see page 156)

Orange bitters

Preheat a mug by filling it with boiling water, and then pour it out. Add the spelt whiskey, and top with the hot chocolate and espresso coffee. Sweeten with the Basic Simple Syrup, spoon the Homemade Whipped Cream over the top, and dot with orange bitters. Bliss!

Old Gnaw

Sometimes, a strong drink is exactly what the doctor ordered. If that's where you're at, look no further than an Old Gnaw. Paired with freshly squeezed lemon juice and a simple syrup made with smoky chiles, it showcases hopped whiskey, which adds a beer-flavored spark to just about any cocktail. Why? Because, while all whiskeys begin life as "beer" (though you wouldn't want to drink it before it becomes whiskey, that's for sure), they're usually made *sans* hops. (Hops are the flowers of the hop plant, and they're used in beermaking to lend your favorite brew its distinctive bitterness—or lack thereof—and its aroma.) Hopped whiskey, on the other hand, *is* made with hops: Hence the name, and the unmistakable beer-like flavor. Then it's aged in American oak barrels for a while, before being bottled and sold. The Old Gnaw, a perfect aperitif, is sure to raise your spirits (no pun intended!) at the end of a long day.

2 ounces (60 ml) **hopped whiskey**

½ ounce (15 ml) **Spicy Simple Syrup (see page 157)**

½ ounce (15 ml) **lemon juice**

1 **egg white**

1 scant pinch **of sea salt**

¼ ounce (7 ml) **club soda**

Dash of grapefruit bitters

Fill a Boston shaker three-quarters full with ice. Add the whiskey, Spicy Simple Syrup, lemon juice, egg white, and sea salt. Shake hard for about 15 seconds. Strain into a coupe glass, top with the club soda, and shake a few drops of grapefruit bitters over the top to finish.

Small White Blossom

The Small White Blossom is my Cocktail Whisperer's take on the classic New Orleans–style Kentucky Whiskey cocktail, which calls for only two ingredients: bourbon and pineapple juice. As usual, I take things a bit further. My version uses craft whiskey made from millet, not bourbon. Its toasted-almond and caramel flavors are a great match for fresh fruit juices. Here, grilled pineapple juice combined with freshly squeezed orange juice gives the Blossom an extra layer of flavor, while a splash of club soda and the tiniest pinch of sea salt add a refreshing, palate-tickling lift. If you can find it, make your simple syrup with gum arabic (also spelled "gomme arabic"), which yields a lush, creamy mouth feel. The result: A cocktail that's small but perfectly formed.

2 ounces (60 ml) **millet whiskey**

1 ounce (30 ml) **Grilled Pineapple Juice (see page 156)**

1 ounce (30 ml) **freshly squeezed orange juice**

½ ounce (15 ml) **Basic Simple Syrup (see page 156) (This version of the simple syrup is made with** 2 tablespoons (30 ml) **gomme arabic for extra thickness (add 1 tablespoon [15 ml] of gum arabic to your Basic Simple Syrup and heat to the desired color and thickness)**

Dash of club soda

Pinch of sea salt

Fill a mixing glass three-quarters full with ice. Add the millet whiskey, fruit juices, and simple syrup. Stir gently, pour into a coupe glass, top with the club soda, and garnish with a narrow spear of grilled pineapple. Add the pinch of sea salt over the top to finish.

German Pavilion Cocktail

One of my favorite drinks takes its inspiration from the German *rauch,* or smoked, beers that I enjoyed as a college student, and this cocktail is named for the German Pavilion at the 1964 World's Fair in New York. Like those strikingly smoky German suds, some alternative-grain whiskeys have such assertive flavors that enjoying them takes some practice. Smoked whiskey—in which the grains themselves are smoked, sometimes using a combination of fuels such as wood and peat—is one of them, and it takes center stage in this cocktail. But herbal, citrusy, Campari-like Sanbitter, an Italian soda with a bright-red hue, is more than a match for smoked whiskey—as is the dash of mezcal that rounds out this minimalist, but mesmerizing, drink. (You can find Sanbitter in specialty food shops.) Serve it in a tall Collins-style glass, with one stick of sparklingly clear hand-cut ice, and watch your guests swoon.

¼ ounce (7 ml) **mezcal**

2 ounces (60 ml) **smoked American whiskey**

1 bottle of **Sanbitter soda (4 ounces, or 120 ml)**

1 thinly sliced **lemon wheel, halved**

Wash a Collins glass with the mezcal, and then pour the mezcal out (into your mouth, perhaps?). Add the smoked whiskey to the washed glass, and top with a chilled bottle of Sanbitter, and garnish with a very thin half-round of lemon. It's supernaturally good.

Ulysses Left on Ithaca Cocktail

Smoked American whiskey is a wonderful match for a citrus-oil–tinged tea like Earl Grey. Don't worry, I'm not suggesting you start spiking your morning pick-me-up; this delicate cocktail proves that Earl Grey isn't just for breakfast anymore. Bound together by homemade ginger simple syrup, the Ulysses delivers spicy, sweet, smoky, and even salty—all at once. This cocktail is named for the Greek hero of the epic poem *The Odyssey*. Reluctant to leave his homeland of Ithaca, he pretended to be insane by sowing his fields with salt instead of grain. In his honor, the final touch to the Ulysses is a pinch of sea salt, which adds an unexpected, crunchy kick. It's a delicious finish. The ingredients for this cocktail are simplicity themselves, but the sum of the parts is truly bewitching.

4 ounces (120 ml) **freshly brewed Earl Grey tea, cooled**

3 ounces (90 ml) **smoked American whiskey**

2 ounces (60 ml) **Spicy Ginger Honey Simple Syrup (see page 157)**

1 ounce (30 ml) **club soda**

2 pinches **of sea salt**

2 sprigs **of thyme**

Brew and cool the Earl Grey tea. Fill a mixing glass three-quarters full with ice. Pour the whiskey, tea, and the Spicy Ginger Honey Simple Syrup over the ice, and then stir to combine. Taste for sweetness: If it's not sweet enough, add a bit more simple syrup. Place a chunk of hand-cut ice into each of two short rocks glasses. (If you really want to bring out the gingery taste of the simple syrup, make ginger ice in advance: Freeze slices of fresh ginger root into your homemade ice.) Add the splash of club soda to each glass, and top each with a pinch of sea salt to add a welcome "crunch" to each sip. Garnish with the thyme sprigs—and get ready to pour a second round.

The Runaway Mountain Train

If you're like me, the mere mention of muddled blueberries makes your mouth water: think plucking sun-warmed wild blueberries straight from the bush and popping them straight into your mouth; think freshly baked blueberry pie topped with vanilla ice cream. Sigh. This cocktail mixes those summertime pleasures with smoky millet whiskey and a fragrant hit of maple syrup for a lightly fizzy drink that's delicious any time of year (although it's best made with wild blueberries, if you can get them!). It's not all syrupy-sugary, though: The club soda, sea salt, and citrus bitters add an edginess and sophistication to the Runaway Mountain Train. That's what makes it so very drinkable. As in life, so in the art of mixology: You need the salt and the bitters to balance the cocktail's luscious sweetness.

¼ cup (35 g) **blueberries (preferably wild Maine blueberries)**

3 ounces (90 ml) **millet whiskey**

1 teaspoon (5 ml) **maple syrup**

Hand-cut ice

2 ounces (60 ml) **club soda**

Pinch of sea salt

Dash of citrus bitters

Muddle the blueberries in a Boston shaker. Add the millet whiskey and the maple syrup. Fill the shaker three-quarters full with ice. Cap and shake for about 15 seconds. Place one cube of hand-cut ice into each of two rocks glasses, and then split the contents of the shaker between the two glasses. Top each with a splash of club soda; add a pinch of sea salt to each; and then finish with a few drops of citrus bitters. Serves 2 parched passengers.

Mr. Strahan's Severed Ear

Craft spirits made from artisan grains often have strong, memorable flavors. An easy way to introduce yourself to the world of alternative-grain whiskeys is to simply pour yourself a measure of your whiskey of choice, and then add a splash of freshly squeezed lemon juice and a little Raw Honey Simple Syrup. It's a kind of instant cocktail, and it's a great way to experiment with new spirits. Once you've fallen in love with spelt whiskey, you'll want to try a tequila-laced Severed Ear. (There's a sentence you won't hear every day.) Named after a fictional seaman who slices off a portion of his own ear, this potent cocktail really packs a punch, thanks to un-aged tequila (a great partner for spelt whiskey) and grilled grapefruit juice, which lends it a subtle, charred flavor. A distant cousin of the tequila sunrise, Mr. Strahan's Severed Ear makes a bracing aperitif.

2 ounces (60 ml) **Casa Noble Joven, or other young, potent, and "moonshine-like" tequila**

1 ounce (30 ml) **spelt whiskey**

2 ounces (60 ml) **Grilled Grapefruit Juice (see page 156)**

1 ounce (30 ml) **Spicy Simple Syrup (try Royal Rose's Simple Syrup of Three Chiles, or make your own: see page 157)**

2 ounces (60 ml) **grapefruit-flavored sparkling natural mineral water**

3 drops **Mexican mole bitters**

Fill a Boston shaker three-quarters full with ice. Add the first four ingredients to the shaker, and shake for about 15 seconds. Pour into a coupe glass, top with the sparkling water, and add the bitters. Serves two. Try not to have more than two rounds of these: If you do, the Cocktail Whisperer will not be responsible for the fate of your own ears.

The Vendetta Cocktail

The inspiration for the Vendetta Cocktail comes from a walk I took through Brooklyn recently. So many of Brooklyn's turn-of-the-century buildings have been demolished, and so many visible memories of the borough's past have been erased during its transformation into the hipster paradise it is today. And it's a huge loss. In order to honor Brooklyn's past, I wanted to combine ingredients from the old neighborhood delis such as Manhattan Special Espresso Coffee Soda and vanilla *gelato* to create this boozy take on the traditional Italian dessert *affogato*, which involves pouring freshly pulled espresso over vanilla ice cream. I like to muddle a few home-cured cocktail cherries into my Vendetta; they help to smooth the smoked whiskey's bold taste. A very grown-up drink, indeed.

3 to 4 **Easy Home-Cured Cocktail Cherries (see page 156)**

2 ounces (60 ml) **smoked American whiskey**

4 ounces (120 ml) **coffee soda, such as Manhattan Special Espresso Coffee Soda**

1 scoop **vanilla *gelato* (or top-quality vanilla ice cream)**

With the back of a bar spoon or the end of a wooden spoon, muddle a couple home-cured cocktail cherries to a pulp in the bottom of a mixing glass. Then add the smoked whiskey, followed by the coffee soda and the gelato. Mix gently with a long spoon, and portion between two coupe glasses. Sprinkle a bit of espresso powder over the top of each drink, if you like. Serves two persone.

White Whiskey

Over the years, white whiskey has earned itself a

bit of a reputation. Unlike whiskeys such as bourbon or Scotch, white whiskey isn't subjected to aging in oak barrels—a process that can take anywhere from a few months to a few years. That means it's ready to drink relatively quickly, right after it's distilled.

Traditionally, white whiskey or moonshine was distilled illegally, often from a recipe of fifty-percent corn and fifty-percent sugar, and it certainly wouldn't have had a very developed flavor profile (or, really, any flavor at all, unless you can call a taste reminiscent of the sound of a screech owl "flavor"). And forget about aging the stuff: Back in the day, during Prohibition, the most aging a typical batch of moonshine got was a fifteen-minute high-speed, cop-dodging car chase. Incredibly high proof and terribly flammable, early moonshine delivered a mule-kick to the drinker's chin after each and every slurp. Sometimes, moonshiners would add ripe, sweet fruit to large Mason jars of "shine" in an attempt to make it passably drinkable. Then, a bit later on, some enterprising 'shiners began to add their hooch to sweet iced tea or sugary lemonade for the same reason. It might have helped mask the hair raising taste, but it didn't make the stuff any less lethal. In the wrong hands, it was, and still is, dangerous stuff. The tippler had to sip moonshine at his or her (usually "his," though) own risk, and it was usually best to follow your mother's time-tested advice: If you don't know where it's been, don't put it in your mouth.

As romantic as homegrown moonshine sounds, either distilling or consuming it is a very, very bad idea. Drinkers sometimes went blind from drinking 'shine from unclean stills, or even died from overconsumption. Today, there's really no such thing as country-distilled moonshine for sale in a licensed liquor store: If a spirit's made using a backyard country still, it's illegal. So don't do it. The Bureau of Alcohol, Tobacco, Firearms and Explosives in the United States considers producing and running unlicensed liquor to be a major crime; you can end up doing serious jail time if you choose to distill liquor illegally. And there's nothing glamorous about that.

The moral of the story is, stick to what's on the shelves of your local liquor store, where the name "moonshine" is strictly a marketing term. And you can rest assured you won't be stuck for choice. Whether you call it white whiskey, clear whiskey, white dog, moonshine, or white lightning, un-aged or "white" whiskey is a fast-growing category. And you'll find that there are delicious, craft-distilled articulations of it available—many of which are even made with alternative grains, like oats and wheat. (Historically, white whiskey was distilled from a variety of things. In places like New Jersey, where apples were grown as a cash crop [and still are], moonshine wasn't far behind. Sammy's Ye Old Cider Mill in Mendham, which began life as a Prohibition-era speakeasy, used to pump their liquor from the apple mill across the street. Take my word for it: Apple-based moonshine is potent stuff!)

Of course, white whiskey isn't a solely American phenomenon. Distilling alcohol from local fruits and grains is an ancient craft that's been thousands of years in the making. We've only to glance around the globe to prove it: Think of highly intoxicating fruit- and grain-based spirits such as Italian *grappa,* South American *pisco,* French *eau de vie,* and, of course, eastern European vodka. Then, enterprising immigrant distillers brought their back yard fermentation knowledge with them on their journeys to the New World. Some of the drinks in this chapter are inspired by these craftspeople.

Oh, and speaking of vodka: Remember, like vodka, white whiskey is clear, but that doesn't mean it is vodka. Although it's often made from similar raw ingredients, vodka is distilled at a different temperature and proof level, and the multiple distillations that vodka undergoes strips the flavor from the grains, resulting in a clear, flavorless spirit. (Those flavored vodkas on the market? Fuhgeddaboutit. I don't even consider them "vodka" at all.) You might be tempted to substitute any clear spirit for the recipes in this chapter— but be strong. Don't do it. Stick with white whiskey when you're preparing these cocktails. I've chosen the flavor combinations carefully and they're not interchangeable with all clear spirits.

On that note, check out my recipe for the Jenks Farm Restorative, which is a big pitcher of hangover featuring heavy cream, white whiskey, and yesterday's black coffee. Or, if it's a quiet retreat you're after, try my Cabin in the Pines Cocktail: Its combination of white whiskey, muddled stone fruits, hit of Fernet Branca, and a dash of bitters will whisk you away to a gentler world. If you're heading out on a summer hike or a beach expedition, it's easy to take The Two-Mile Cocktail along in a thermos, since it's a tipsy version of iced tea topped up with white whiskey and a bit of absinthe. Then look upwards, and ask, "Where's the Dog Star?" It's a simple cocktail of homemade frozen hot chocolate, root tea liquor, and white whiskey—the best of all possible threesomes.

Read on to discover more recipes for working white whiskey into your mixological repertoire.

Note to the Reader:

All recipes make a single serving, unless otherwise indicated.

The Jenks Farm Restorative

We've all had those mornings: You had one too many cocktails the night before, you finally hit the sack at some unknown but ungodly hour, and now your stressed-out belly can't stomach your usual cup of coffee—or, heaven help us, food. That's where The Jenks Farm Restorative, a powerful breakfast-time cocktail, comes in. It's a healing concoction of white whiskey and iced coffee laced with heavy cream and sweet vanilla syrup, served over crushed ice—and it's best made by the pitcherful, because it goes down so very quickly and easily. The moonshine provides a little hair of the proverbial dog, while the chilled coffee gets much-needed caffeine into your system, fast. Don't skip the freshly grated nutmeg—inhaling nutmeg's warm, heady scent is like aromatherapy for hangover sufferers.

6 ounces (175 ml) **white whiskey**

8 ounces (235 ml) **heavy cream**

6 ounces (175 ml) **whole milk**

4 ounces (120 ml) **Basic Simple Syrup (see page 156)** mixed with 2 teaspoons **real vanilla extract,** or to taste

6 ounces (175 ml) **old black coffee (yesterday morning's coffee is fine), chilled**

Freshly scraped nutmeg

Combine the first five ingredients in a 32-ounce (1 L) pitcher, and stir well. Fill rocks glasses with crushed ice, and (quickly!) pour this toothsome restorative over the ice. Grate some fresh nutmeg over each drink, and sip to the good health of friends both near and far. Serves 4 aching heads.

Sleepy Time Down South of Broad

Back in the 1980s, I lived in Charleston, South Carolina, where I enjoyed my very first sip of bourbon. Later on, I tasted my first mint julep, made with care in an antique silver cup. The sensation of that drink's icy, refreshing chill against the steamy Charleston night has stayed with me to this day—and it's what's inspired the Sleepy Time Down South of Broad cocktail. This tipple reads like your traditional mint julep—but it takes a sharp right turn off Tradd Street and heads down South of Broad, since it calls for white whiskey instead of the traditional bourbon. And if you haven't slapped your fresh mint before, you should start now: Remove mint leaves from their bitter stem, place them in one hand, and slap your other hand against it. This releases mint's aromatic oils, without actually chopping or tearing it. So get slapping, and start mixing.

2 tablespoons (30 g) **"slapped" fresh mint**

1 tablespoon (15 g) **raw sugar**

3 ounces (90 ml) **white whiskey**

Crushed ice

Sterling silver julep cup, freshly polished

Muddle 1 tablespoon (15 ml) of the slapped mint with half of the sugar in the bottom of the silver cup to release the mint's fragrant oils (with a non-metal utensil, preferably; never use stainless metal against sterling silver, ever!). Add about half of the white whiskey and some crushed ice to the cup, and mix. Then add more ice, the rest of the sugar, the rest of the white whiskey, and the rest of the mint; stir gently until your cup is frosty and glistening. True Southern hospitality dictates that you serve one to a friend before serving yourself. That's one thing Charleston herself taught me.

Captain Swank's Sandwich Sippah

This long drink will add a touch of class to just about any casual meal. It's simple: Just ditch the boring corn syrup–based sodas in favor of this kicked-up cousin of the rum 'n' cola. The Captain Swank is definitely on the sweet side, but the maple syrup adds a woody depth of flavor to this cocktail; the very picture of versatility, it is muscular enough to stand up to even the most robust flavors. Try it alongside just about any sandwich—a bacon-laden club sandwich made with good bread and straight-off-the-vine tomatoes, or a blue-cheeseburger laced with caramelized onions and a handful of fries. If you ask me, though, it's hard to beat slices of bourbon-glazed ham and plenty of Dijon mustard on excellent bread. (See my recipe for Bourbon and Maple Syrup Glazed Ham and Swiss Sandwiches on page 148.) Go all out and make your own potato chips to go alongside—it's worth it.

2 ounces (60 ml) **white whiskey**

4 ounces (120 ml) **cane sugar–based sarsaparilla soda**

1 tablespoon (15 ml) **maple syrup**

Easy Home-Cured Cocktail Cherry (see page 156), for garnish

Lime zest twist

Ice

Place one long spear of hand-cut ice, or 2 ice cubes, in a Collins glass. Pour the white whiskey over the ice, and then add the sarsaparilla soda and the maple syrup. Stir gently. Squeeze a lime chunk into the drink, and garnish with a lime zest twist and an Easy Home-Cured Cocktail Cherry. Serve immediately. Guaranteed to brighten up any lunchtime.

Cabin in the Pines Cocktail

When the dirty old world gets to be just a little too much, it's time to escape for a while. Stage a retreat from the rat race, and mix yourself a Cabin in the Pines. Here, stone fruits like peaches and plums become extra-luscious when slow-roasted in the oven: They assume otherworldly shapes and colors, their sweet, summery flavors become concentrated and intensified, and viscous juices flow from deep within their shriveled flesh. When muddled and mixed with white whiskey, these roasted fruits become magical stuff. Add a bit of club soda and a splash of Fernet Branca for health (they're very belly-friendly, so if you're suffering the aftereffects of a five-course meal or a few too many margaritas, help is on the way!) and you've got a restorative of the highest order.

2 heaping tablespoons (30 g) **Roasted Stone Fruits (see page 157)**

2 ounces (60 ml) **white whiskey**

½ ounce (15 ml) **Fernet Branca**

2 ounces (60 ml) **Raw Honey Simple Syrup (see page 157)**

1 ounce (30 ml) **club soda**

2 to 3 drops **aromatic bitters**

Add the roasted stone fruits to a Boston shaker, and using the back of a bar spoon or the end of a wooden spoon, muddle them to release their juices. Then, add the white whiskey, the Fernet Branca, and the Raw Honey Simple Syrup. Fill the shaker three-quarters full with ice and shake for about 15 seconds. Strain into a coupe glass, and top with a splash of the club soda. Finish with a couple drops of aromatic bitters of your choice.

Bill Monroe's Kentucky Cooler

I can only imagine the various kinds of liquor that may—or may not—have been served in the early days of bluegrass legend Bill Monroe's career as a performer. After all, the Kentucky mandolinist was active in the years just before Prohibition ended, and I'm sure folks didn't always stick to sweet iced tea or milk while listening to his music! As tart and sweet as bluegrass itself, this cocktail balances white whiskey with lush peach and apricot nectars, plus a dose of iced tea and a dash of bitters. Of course, it's just the thing for sipping on a long summer's evening—but truth be told, it's wonderful any time of the year.

1 ounce (30 ml) **peach nectar**

1 ounce (30 ml) **apricot nectar**

½ ounce (15 ml) **lemon juice**

2 ounces (60 ml) **sweet iced tea**

2 ounces (60 ml) **white whiskey**

2 to 3 shakes **Angostura bitters**

Fill a mixing glass three-quarters full with ice. Add the fruit juices and the sweet iced tea, and then the white whiskey. Mix gently and carefully. Place a few hand-cut ice cubes into a Collins glass, and pour the mixture over the ice. Top with a few drops of bitters, and serve with a colorful straw!

Chamois Cloth Shake

No matter how sophisticated you might be, you're never too cool for a milkshake. Especially when that milkshake is, in essence, a Creamsicle for grownups. As soft and smooth as its eponymous chamois cloth, this chilled-out cocktail spikes orange sorbet with white whiskey and a soupçon of rosemary-infused simple syrup, which lends it a woody, elegant edge. The result is a soothing, cooling libation that takes seconds to whip up—and it acts as an astoundingly effective hangover cure.

2 ounces (60 ml) **white whiskey**

2 small scoops **orange gelato**

4 ounces (120 ml) **whole milk**

2 to 3 **ice cubes**

1 tablespoon (15 ml) **Rosemary Simple Syrup (see page 157)**

Add all the ingredients to a blender, and blend until well combined. Serve the Chamois in a Collins glass with a long straw—for slurping up every last drop.

The Two-Mile Cocktail

This thermos-friendly cocktail for two was inspired by a halcyon trip I took one summer, out the Two-Mile Hollow Lane on the east end of New York State's Long Island. It's an easily transportable slurp, and it's simply made, with only a handful of ingredients, including white whiskey, absinthe, peach nectar, and cooled jasmine tea. Once you make a batch, you can just pour it into an insulated flask or thermos, pop said thermos into your backpack alongside your provisions, and head for the beach. The Two-Mile packs a wallop, though, so be sure to share with a friend or it'll sweep you out to sea, guaranteed. Forget the sugar-laden, frat-boy cocktail most bars call the Long Island Iced Tea; this Long Island–inspired tipple is the real deal.

4 ounces (120 ml) **white whiskey**

½ ounce (15 ml) **absinthe**

8 ounces (235 ml) **brewed jasmine tea, cooled (not jasmine *green* tea—that's a different beast)**

3 shakes **Peychaud's bitters**

3 ounces (90 ml) **peach nectar, preferably organic**

Add all the ingredients to a Boston shaker filled three-quarters full with ice, and shake like crazy for about 15 seconds. (You may have to do this in two batches.) Strain into your insulated flask, and you're ready to go. Head out into the sun with a friend—and be sure to bring straws!

Roaming Hound Dog Cocktail

White whiskey—also known as "white dog"—is a versatile spirit indeed, and it's especially delicious when paired with that toothsome Asian concoction known as bubble tea. Traditionally meant to accompany Vietnamese cuisine, bubble tea is a blend of coconut milk, ice, tapioca pearls, and sweet fruit or tea. While you can buy it at most Asian supermarkets, it's easy to make at home. My version calls for pureed tropical fruits, like starfruit, Asian pears, jackfruits, and oranges, plus a dose of white whiskey and a little good-quality dark rum. If you can, use rhum agricole: Its intense sugar-cane flavor is delicious against the icy creaminess of coconut milk and coconut cream. The Roaming Hound Dog isn't all bark and no bite, though. If you indulge in more than one, you might find yourself begging for the hair of the dog the next morning.

2 ounces (60 ml) **white whiskey**

¼ ounce (7 ml) **dark rum**

2 tablespoons (30 g) **Luscious Asian Fruit Puree (see page 157)**

½ cup (120 ml) **coconut milk**

¼ cup (60 ml) **sweetened coconut cream**

Crushed ice

¼ cup (60 ml) **brewed, cooled jasmine tea**

1 tablespoon (15 g) **cooked tapioca pearls**

Pour the white whiskey and dark rum into a blender. Then add the fruit puree, coconut milk, and coconut cream, along with a few handfuls of crushed ice and the jasmine tea. Blend until smooth. Toss the tapioca pearls into a tall glass, and pour a large measure of the Roaming Hound Dog mixture over them. Use a colorful, wide-mouthed straw to suck up each succulent pearl. It's heaven in a glass.

Where's the Dog Star?

This simple cocktail features three of my favorite ingredients: white whiskey, organic root tea liqueur, and frozen hot chocolate. With its crunchy, slushy texture, Where's the Dog Star? is more than a mere tipple: It's also a healing tonic of the highest order. That's because root tea liqueur is a combination of hand-selected medicinal spices and extracts of healing roots, suspended and preserved in alcohol. Add a healthy dose of white whiskey to the mix, plus some homemade frozen hot chocolate, and you've got a fortifying cocktail that'll keep your spirits up despite blustery weather and howling gales. Try it on its own on a stormy afternoon; as a dessert (in all weathers); or, best of all, as a nightcap. It's a fabulous restorative for both body and soul.

3 ounces (90 ml) **The Best Hot Chocolate (see page 156), frozen and crushed into pebbles**

2 ounces (60 ml) **white whiskey**

1 ounce (30 ml) **organic root tea liqueur**

Prepare the Best Hot Chocolate, and let it cool a little. Pour into an ice-cube tray, and freeze 8 hours or overnight. Pop the hot chocolate ice cubes into a blender and crush, or place them into a Lewis bag—a canvas bag especially made for crushing ice—and crush by hand by banging them with a wooden mallet. (It's actually a lot of fun!) Spoon the crushed, frozen hot chocolate into a parfait glass, and then add the white whiskey and the root tea liqueur. Mix gently. Serve with both a straw and a long-handled spoon.

Packing the Old Pickup Truck

This memorable, white whiskey–laden cocktail was inspired by the quince fruit grown on my family's farm, down past the apple orchards. A late-season fruit that's usually ripe by November, quince looks like the offspring of an apple and a pear, and it's a bright lemon yellow. Fresh quince isn't terribly pretty to look at, but when roasted, it's absolutely sublime: It has a faint citrus flavor, and it's tinged with the restrained elegance of light stone fruits. After spending some time in a hot oven, the natural sugars in the quince ooze out, and it becomes a wonderful addition to cocktails like the Old Pickup Truck. You can find quince in specialty food shops or, in season, at your local farmer's market—but feel free to use store-bought quince paste instead. Combined with *raki* (a strong Turkish aniseed liqueur), club soda, and a hint of orange flower water, this cocktail is sophisticated and exotic, all at once.

3 ounces (90 ml) **white whiskey**

1 ounce (30 ml) *raki*

3 ounces (85 g) **Quince Puree (see page 157), or store-bought quince paste**

2 ounces (60 ml) **Raw Honey Simple Syrup (see page 157)**

1 ounce (30 ml) **club soda**

Very small dash of orange flower water

Hand-cut ice

Add the first four ingredients to a Boston shaker filled three-quarters full with ice. Shake hard for about 15 seconds. Place a chunk of hand-cut ice into a rocks glass, and strain the mixture into the glass. Top with the club soda and the orange flower water, and, if you like, garnish with an orange pinwheel. Serves two quinceheads.

Rye Whiskey

Happily, rye whiskey is making a comeback.

Although it fell out of favor with American drinkers in the last half of the twentieth century, today it's enjoying a full-fledged renaissance. In the past decade, craft distillers around the United States, many of whom are eager to revive the historical rye distilling traditions from regions like the Midwest or New York State, have embraced rye with open arms. And when it comes to cocktails, the palates of *bon vivants* are expanding: Drinkers aren't craving the super-sweet stuff as much these days, and they're getting turned on by rye's dry, spicy flavor profile. It's official: Rye whiskey is back on the menu, and for proof, you needn't look further than your favorite cocktail bar's menu, where, I'd hazard, a well-made Old-Fashioned and a classic Manhattan get top billing. And that shouldn't come as a surprise, since rye whiskey's history is a long and august one, as old as America itself. While rum was the first spirit to be distilled in pre-Revolutionary America, the raw materials for making it had to be imported from the West Indies.

When British blockades cut off the supply of these ingredients, distillers were forced to turn to grains to produce spirits. Luckily for drinkers of days gone by, rye is a tough old bird, and it thrives in colder climates: for instance, the Northeast of the United States. Soon, farmers were converting their surplus grain into whiskey, which, along with rum, was actually used as currency for a time, before the establishment of a central bank. Early rye whiskey was probably quite a bit rougher than today's rye. Nonetheless, these liquid investments (no pun intended!) were extremely useful. Unlike beer or wine, spirits are durable stuff, easy to strap onto the back of a wagon (no shock absorbers necessary) or sling over the back of a mule. There's no doubt about it: Early rye whiskey satisfied a thirsty population in a way few other beverages could.

Today, there are strict regulations governing the production of rye whiskey. Rye whiskeys are made from at least fifty-one percent rye and must be aged in new charred-oak barrels. (Some distilleries are experimenting with whiskeys that are made from up to 100-percent rye.) In order for a rye whiskey to be classified as "straight" rye, it must be aged for a minimum of two years and can't contain any additional flavorings or colorings. And in terms of flavor, rye is a very different beast to its corn-based cousins, such as bourbon. To me, rye has almost an acrid, smoky taste, which quickly develops into a mouth-drying, cinnamony finish. It's far less sweet and far drier than corn-based whiskeys, with a sharp acidity that doesn't appeal to all drinkers. But it's that very acidity that makes it a great match for food. Rye whiskey is an excellent accompaniment to salted and cured meats, such as pastrami and corned beef. (After all, they're both traditionally served on rye bread for a reason!) Rye also complements the yellow mustard–heavy Southern barbeque. And it's great with just about anything that's been slowly smoked over hardwood charcoal, a technique that echoes the smoky spiciness inherent in rye whiskey.

The recipes in this chapter will show you how to make the most of the rye whiskey revival—and they'll show you how versatile rye really is. In the past, rye's been mostly mixed with sweet sodas, or—for the really brave— taken neat. My cocktails are much more creative. Rye's spiciness is a delicious match for fresh fruit juices (even grapefruit!) and for concentrated, flavored simple syrups. It also goes famously with spicy hot chocolate.

There are, literally, thousands of possibilities for rye-based cocktails, and some of the very best of them are right here. If you consider yourself a bit of a purist when it comes to rye, head straight for an Old-Fashioned. My Cocktail Whisperer's version calls for top-notch bitters and a flamed orange peel, which lends an intensity of flavor that complements rye's trademark spiciness. Or, if you're feeling adventurous already, try my Slightly Askew Old-Fashioned, which turns that classic drink on its head by mixing rye with Fernet Branca, sage tea, and Mexican mole bitters. Stick with the Fernet Branca if it's a rye-friendly *digestif* you're after, and mix up a Pleasant Little Gentleman: It's a savory-yet-sweet hot toddy that combines rye, Fernet, and a heavy pour of strong black tea, and there's no better way to finish a hearty winter meal. (Trust me: I speak from experience.) And since all things charred, roasted, and smoked are natural matches for rye whiskey, my Rye Slushee with Roasted Strawberries and Rhubarb Tea is a winner when it comes to summertime sipping: The caramelized fruit brings out the rye's spiciness, and a dash of club soda and a pinch of sea salt make it a real palate tickler.

And the most important thing to remember when it comes to the art of mixology: relax. As thirsty as you and your guests might be, take your time making each drink, and enjoy the process as you build each layer of flavor into a cocktail. It's worth it! Read on to get inspired by the rye revolution.

Note to the Reader:

All recipes make a single serving,
unless otherwise indicated.

The Classic Old-Fashioned

The main ingredient in a perfectly crafted Old-Fashioned cocktail is love. Sure, there's been a lot of disagreement among mixologists in recent years over the recipe: lots of fruit, or no fruit at all? Whichever camp you might be in, the keys to a great Old-Fashioned—a drink that's truly an integral part of American cocktail culture—are patience and passion. My version calls for a slice of thickly cut orange rind, instead of the traditional chunks of citrus fruit; singeing the rind with a lit match releases its aromatic essential oils, soaking the sugar cube with flavor. And the bitters are an important component of this drink, so feel free to experiment a bit. There are so many different varieties on the market these days—and some yield fascinating results! I enjoy the process of making an Old-Fashioned almost as much as I enjoy sipping one.

1 rough-cut **brown sugar cube**

2 dashes **aromatic bitters of your choice**

2 ounces (60 ml) **rye whiskey**

1 thickly cut **orange zest twist (use a paring knife, not a peeler)**

Hand-cut ice cubes

Place the sugar cube in an old-fashioned glass. Wet the cube with the aromatic bitters. Singe the orange zest twist by holding it firmly behind a lit match and pinching it to release its natural citrus oils. Be careful to spritz the citrus oils into the glass. Place the orange zest twist into the glass; using a muddler or the end of a wooden spoon, press it gently against the sugar cube. Then add the rye whiskey and stir gently. Add a couple large hand-cut ice cubes to the glass; stir gently again. Garnish with another orange zest twist, and serve. It's restrained, potable elegance in a glass.

Slightly Askew Old-Fashioned

You're familiar with the Classic Old-Fashioned. Now, here's the Cocktail Whisperer's twisted take on it! After all, not to experiment with the Old-Fashioned paradigm would be a crime against creativity. At first glance, this cocktail may seem a bit on the complicated side, but it's actually a snap to make. In addition to rye whiskey and belly-friendly Fernet, my version of the Old-Fashioned involves organic sage tea liqueur, which is a distinctive American liquor made from a combination of restorative herbs. Instead of using a flamed orange zest twist, I make this cocktail Slightly Askew by using orange wedges that have been soaked in Earl Grey tea overnight. Italian vermouth brings up the rear here, while the Mexican mole bitters lend the drink an earthy simplicity. The finished product is a combination of flavors that's just astonishing.

1 **orange,** cut into 1-inch (2.5-cm) wedges and **soaked overnight in Earl Grey**

1 ounce (30 ml) **rye whiskey**

1 ounce (30 ml) **Fernet Branca**

¼ ounce (7 ml) **Italian vermouth**

¼ ounce (7 ml) **organic sage tea liqueur**

3 drops **Mexican mole bitters, or aromatic bitters**

Easy Home-Cured Cocktail Cherries (see page 156)

Place two Earl Grey–soaked orange segments in the bottom of a Boston shaker. Add the rye whiskey, then muddle with a muddler or the end of a wooden spoon. Add the Fernet Branca, Italian vermouth, and sage tea liqueur. Then fill the shaker three-quarters full with ice. Shake for about 15 seconds. Place a couple of large ice cubes in a rocks glass, and strain the mixture into the glass. Drip the bitters into the glass, and garnish with an Easy Home-Cured Cocktail Cherry. Quite a newfangled take on an old-fashioned classic!

The Classic Whiskey Sour

According to legend, while the author Ernest Hemingway was living in France, he used whiskey sours as a substitute for medicine. He was a man who—to use a gross understatement—knew his liquor, and I tend to agree with him. Well, on this point, at least. Anyway, I've made whiskey sours for years now, and I used to love them with bourbon—but then I discovered that it makes much more sense to use rye in this classic drink. That's because rye whiskey's natural spiciness makes for a drier cocktail. For an alternative take on the whiskey sour, try adding a few drops of bright-red Peychaud's bitters as a final touch; they look gorgeous when dashed over the drink's snow-white foam, and they lend depth and balance to this sweet-and-sour libation.

1 piece **thickly sliced lemon zest**

1 **egg white**

1½ ounces (45 ml) **rye whiskey**

1 ounce (30 ml) **Basic Simple Syrup (see page 156)**

¾ ounce (22 ml) **freshly squeezed lemon juice**

Easy Home-Cured Cocktail Cherry (see page 156)

1 chunk **lemon**

Rub the inside of a cocktail shaker with the lemon zest, and then add the egg white. Dry shake—that is, shake without adding ice—for about 10 seconds to create the meringue-like foam that's essential to a whiskey sour. Then fill the shaker three-quarters full with ice. Add the rye whiskey, simple syrup, and lemon juice. Shake for another 10 seconds or so. Strain the mixture into an old-fashioned glass, and garnish with the lemon chunk and an Easy Home-Cured Cocktail Cherry. Magnificent.

The Pretty-Close-to-Normal Manhattan

Since it's a twentieth-century classic, you're probably already familiar with the Manhattan, at least in theory. Perhaps your mom drank one on the rocks every evening before dinner. Or maybe your beer-loving great-uncle used to mix himself a straight-up Manhattan once in awhile, on special occasions. Just like Mom and Great-Uncle Harold, the Manhattan is one of my favorite "normal" cocktails (for "normal," read "un–Cocktail Whisperified"). Its ingredients are as simple as could be, and it's just as easy to prepare. Aside from the rye whiskey, there's nothing at all to add but bitters and sweet vermouth—but do feel free to play the field when it comes to the vermouth. I prefer Italian sweet vermouth, but you may like the French variety, or even a herbaceous American version. Whichever way you craft your Manhattan, as long as you make it with rye whiskey, all will be well.

2 ounces (60 ml) **rye whiskey**

½ ounce (15 ml) **sweet vermouth**

Several shakes of **aromatic bitters**

Easy Home-Cured Cocktail Cherry (see page 156)

Fill a cocktail mixing glass three-quarters full with ice. Add the rye whiskey, vermouth, and a few shakes of the aromatic bitters. Stir well, and then strain into either a rocks glass or a martini glass. (Some people add ice at this point, but I am not one of them.) Add an Easy Home-Cured Cocktail Cherry to finish. Serve one to an appreciative friend—then mix up another one for yourself. Beware, though: You may have to repeat the process several times!

Rye and Cider Mulligatawny Cocktail

The Rye and Cider Mulligatawny Cocktail takes its inspiration from the way in which cocktails were made in America's early days. Then, as now, apples were an important crop for the Northeastern states, and whiskey—usually rye whiskey—was the only tipple available to the average drinker. Rye whiskey would have been added to apple cider to give it a bit of kick, a combination that lives on in this cocktail. As usual, though, there's a twist: Curry bitters (or, in a pinch, curry powder added to "regular" aromatic bitters) is a tip of the hat to a warm, spicy bowl of mulligatawny stew, which features both apples and curry. Sound weird? It isn't. Dry, spicy rye is the perfect foil to sweet apples—and the curry bitters bind it all together beautifully.

1 apple, preferably one with crisp flesh such as a Macintosh or a Macoun, sliced thickly and seared on a cast-iron pan until soft, but not mushy

½ teaspoon **absinthe**

2 ounces (60 ml) **rye whiskey**

¼ ounce (7 ml) **Italian sweet vermouth**

1 ounce (30 ml) **hard apple cider (or apple brandy, or calvados [a type of apple brandy from the Normandy region of France])**

4 drops **curry bitters (alternatively, use your basic aromatic bitters, and add a very small pinch of curry powder)**

Hand-cut ice cube

Muddle a couple of grilled, softened apple slices with the absinthe in an old-fashioned glass. Add the ice, rye whiskey, and the sweet vermouth. Then add the apple cider or apple brandy, and drip the curry bitters over the top of the glass for a spicy, savory, mulligatawny finish. Here's to rye's venerable history!

Twenty-Cubic-Feet of Sail

As the old song goes, there's nothing like a fresh'ning breeze. Well, there's no doubt about it: This bracing cocktail is sure to put wind in your sails. It matches dry, spicy rye whiskey with an organic ginger liqueur that's reminiscent of old-fashioned gingerbread—the kind made with plenty of fresh ginger and lashings of blackstrap molasses. (Use a good organic ginger liqueur; you won't want to adulterate this cocktail with anything sugary and sickly sweet.) Then a dose of fresh lemon juice supplies a citrusy edge, while seltzer and bitters give the whole shebang a fizzy lift. I think it's a great way to boost a flagging appetite, so try serving a round of Twenty-Cubic-Feet of Sail alongside *hors d'oeuvres* to get your next dinner party off to a rousing start. Anchors aweigh!

2 ounces (60 ml) **rye whiskey**

½ ounce (15 ml) **organic ginger liqueur**

½ ounce (15 ml) **freshly squeezed lemon juice**

4 ounces (120 ml) **seltzer**

Aromatic bitters

Add a couple hand-cut ice cubes to a Collins glass. Pour the rye whiskey over the ice, and then add the ginger liqueur, followed by the lemon juice. Stir gently with a cocktail spoon to combine. Top with the seltzer, and finish with a dash or two of the aromatic bitters. Serve with a straw.

Professor Meiklejohn's Pinky

Named for a professor made famous for his relationship with the writer Robert Louis Stevenson, this rye whiskey–based cold-weather cocktail is sure to restore and inspire. And the best part: It's really easy to prepare. Whip up a batch of the Best Hot Chocolate so it can play host to organic root tea liqueur, rye, and—since this drink really has a flair for the dramatic—a pinch of cayenne pepper. It's a very grown-up version of every kid's favorite wintertime treat. Serve after dinner alongside a plateful of simple, buttery cookies, like homemade madeleines. Or, mix yourself a sneaky Pinky on Christmas morning—no one but you will know that there's a little something extra in your cup of joy. Oh, and be sure to preheat your mug with boiling water beforehand to ensure that your Pinky stays toasty warm.

1 ounce (30 ml) **rye whiskey**

½ ounce (15 ml) **organic root tea liqueur**

3 ounces (90 ml) **The Best Hot Chocolate (see page 156)**

Tiny pinch **cayenne pepper**

1 ounce (30 ml) **Basic Simple Syrup (see page 156)**

1 dash **orange bitters**

Preheat your favorite ceramic mug by filling it with boiling water, and then pour the water out. Add the rye whiskey, root tea liqueur, and then top them with The Best Hot Chocolate. Now add the Basic Simple Syrup—about 1 ounce (30 ml), or to taste—and the cayenne pepper. Finish with a dash or two of orange bitters. Lift your mug in a toast to the Professor.

A Quarter Apiece Cocktail

Thanks to the natural astringency of the quince fruit, rye whiskey and quince is a delicious (and highly effective) pairing. Quince, a late-season tree fruit, is brutally bitter when tasted straight off the tree, and worse, it's hard as stone. (Don't make the mistake of biting into one: Your teeth may end up buried in the fruit for good.) But when it's slow-roasted at a low temperature for a few hours, it's completely transformed. It turns into a tart-sweet mush that works well in a cocktail with rye whiskey, fresh sage, and apple juice (the apple is the quince's first cousin). After you've made your quince puree (or bought it—store-bought quince paste works fine in this drink), the Quarter Apiece isn't hard to make—and plus, you get to set stuff on fire. Smoking fresh sage in your Boston shaker infuses the drink with an inimitable, savory-charred scent that gently perfumes this classy cocktail.

1 small bunch **of fresh sage**

2 ounces (60 ml) **rye whiskey**

½ ounce (15 ml) **botanical gin**

1 ounce (30 ml) **apple juice**

2 ounces (60 ml) **Quince Puree (see page 157), or store-bought quince paste**

½ ounce (15 ml) **club soda**

Several dashes **rhubarb bitters**

Pre-chill a martini glass by filling it with crushed ice and cold water, and then pour the ice water out. Place the sage in a fireproof metal or ceramic bowl. Using a match or lighter, carefully set the sage on fire so that it smokes and smolders. Take a Boston shaker and hold it upside down over the burning sage, so that the shaker's interior is filled with the sweet, sticky smoke. Turn the shaker right-side up, and add the rye whiskey, the gin, and the apple juice. Then, fill the shaker three-quarters full with ice, add the quince puree, and shake for about 20 seconds. Pour the mixture into the martini glass, top with the club soda, and finish with a few dashes of rhubarb bitters.

Revenge of the Painkiller

Rye whiskey is fabulous in drinks that are traditionally made with rum, including my Cocktail Whisperer's riff on the classic Painkiller. A famously dangerous drink that hails from the British islands in the Caribbean, your average, everyday Painkiller consists of rum, pineapple juice, orange juice, and cream of coconut. But, if you ask me, the ingredients in my version are far more interesting. Here, rye whiskey binds espresso, rum, coffee liqueur, and chocolate liqueur together in a lip-smacking concoction that's very effective when sipped just before lunch in the hot sun, on the prow of a yacht, or beside a swimming pool. (Do pre-chill your glassware with crushed ice before serving: Revenge is a drink best served iced.) This lush cocktail is built for two, so share it with someone special. Otherwise, the Painkiller has a tendency to bite back.

2 shots **freshly pulled, cooled espresso coffee**

½ ounce (15 ml) **coffee liqueur**

1 ounce (30 ml) **chocolate liqueur**

½ ounce (15 ml) **dark rum**

1 ounce (30 ml) **rye whiskey**

2 ounces (60 ml) **Basic Simple Syrup (see page 156)**

4 drops **Aztec bitters**

Crushed ice

Freshly scraped nutmeg

Easy Home-Cured Cocktail Cherries (see page 156)

Add all the liquid ingredients and the crushed ice to a blender, and pulse until smooth. Pour the mixture into pre-chilled pint glasses, and scrape some fresh nutmeg over the top. (Avoid the pre-ground stuff—fresh nutmeg is so much better!) Garnish each drink with an Easy Home-Cured Cocktail Cherry, and serve with straws.

Late Summer Fizz

This refreshing, rye-based cocktail is just the thing to whet your appetite before a good lunch on a late summer's day. In addition to rye, it features Pimm's No. 1 Cup, the citrusy-spicy English liqueur that is most agreeable when served with fresh juices and Caribbean spices. That's where allspice dram, a liqueur flavored with allspice berries, comes in: Along with the Pimm's, it gives the drink a dark-red stain that's decidedly preppy (it's the exact color of Nantucket Red trousers). If all this sounds terribly exotic, never fear: Rye whiskey and apple cider, that familiar, time-honored combo, are at the heart of this cocktail. An easy-to-make, uncomplicated tipple, there's one tried-and-true way to drink the Late Summer Fizz that I wholeheartedly recommend: with two long straws, and a great deal of relish.

2 ounces (60 ml) **rye whiskey**

½ ounce (15 ml) **Pimm's No.1 Cup**

½ ounce (15 ml) **non-alcoholic apple cider**

Splash of club soda

¼ ounce (7 ml) **allspice dram**

½ ounce (15 ml) **sweet white Italian vermouth**

Dash of lemon bitters

Pinch of sea salt

Fill a Boston shaker three-quarters full with ice. Add the rye whiskey, the Pimm's, and the cider. Shake for 20 seconds. Pour the mixture over a couple hand-cut ice cubes in an old-fashioned glass, and top with a splash of club soda. Float the allspice dram and the Italian vermouth on top of the drink, and then add the dash of lemon bitters. Finish with a pinch of sea salt for a savory kick.

A Pleasant Little Gentleman

A Pleasant Little Gentleman makes an excellent companion. This warming, tummy-taming toddy is a lovely way to finish a long day. Try one just before bedtime: I can't think of better way to relax than with a steaming Gentleman and a good book. This cocktail combines that famous *digestif,* Fernet Branca, with a dose of rye whiskey, and then sweetens the deal with a simple syrup made from raw honey. In conjunction with the rye and Fernet, raw honey's naturally salubrious enzymes do wonderful things for your uneasy belly—and for your flagging spirits. Sip it from a vintage teacup: That way, the Pleasant Little Gentleman will look just like a regular old cup of tea to the casual observer. The only person who'll know that you're actually taking a healthy sup of something much stronger is you.

2 ounces (60 ml) **Fernet Branca**

1 ounce (30 ml) **rye whiskey**

1 ounce (30 ml) **Raw Honey Simple Syrup (see page 157)**

2 to 3 shakes **whiskey barrel-aged bitters**

Boiling water or very hot black tea (optional)

Preheat a teacup by filling it with boiling water, and then pour the water out. Add the Fernet Branca, the rye whiskey, and the Raw Honey Simple Syrup. Stir gently. Add a couple dashes of the whiskey barrel bitters. The Pleasant Little Gentleman is now ready to serve—but I recommend topping it up with a dose of either boiling water or strong black tea.

Rye Whiskey Slushee
with Roasted Strawberries

Strawberry and rhubarb is a combination that just smacks of summer. But there's no need to wait for those long July evenings to indulge in one of these slushy, R-rated cocktails: This icy drink is refreshing—and bewitching—just about any time of year. Here, organic rhubarb tea liqueur, simultaneously tart and sweet, acts as a tasty counterpoint to caramelized strawberries, and rye whiskey is the boozy glue that binds them together. Like rye whiskey itself, rhubarb has a history that's as old as the United States, and then some: In the eighteenth century, American pharmacists would have recommended it as a digestive aid (as Asian herbal healers had been doing for thousands of years). Plus, rhubarb packs a hefty wallop of vitamin C, which boosts the immune system. So don't wait: Mix up a Rye Whiskey Slushee for a tantalizing taste of days gone by.

2 tablespoons (30 ml) **Roasted Strawberries (see page 157)**

2 ounces (60 ml) **rye whiskey**

1 ounce (30 ml) **organic rhubarb tea liqueur**

1 ounce (30 ml) **Basic Simple Syrup (see page 156)**

Club soda

Pinch of sea salt

Soft, slushy crushed ice

Add the Roasted Strawberries to a Boston shaker. Using a muddler or the end of a wooden spoon, muddle them to release their perfume. Add the rye whiskey, rhubarb tea, and the Basic Simple Syrup. Shake for 20 seconds or so, and strain the mixture into a coupe glass filled half full with the slushy ice. Top with a splash or two of club soda, and a pinch of sea salt.

Other Assorted Tales of Woe

You've probably enjoyed a Dark and Stormy cocktail at some point in your drinking life. It's usually made with a popular, brand name black rum from Bermuda and a very recognizable Bermudan ginger beer, and it has a sweet and sassy personality. You might be familiar with Dark and Stormy weather, but I bet you've never immersed yourself in Assorted Tales of Woe. This variation on the D-and-S theme replaces the black rum with rye whiskey and mixes it with spicy, cane sugar–based ginger beer, plus a shot of thickly sweet, Cuban-style espresso coffee. It's a great pick-me-up for those fuzzy-headed days when you can't decide whether to have a cocktail or a coffee. Now, you can mix business with pleasure and have them both at once. And I guarantee the Tales of Woe will change the way you think about rye whiskey—for the better, of course.

4 ounces (120 ml) **rye whiskey**

1 ounce (30 ml) **freshly squeezed lime juice**

1 ounce (30 ml) **freshly squeezed lemon juice**

2 ounces (60 ml) **sweetened, Cuban-style espresso, cooled:** combine 1 ounce (30 ml) of **espresso** with 1 ounce (30 ml) **Basic Simple Syrup (see page 156)**

4 ounces (120 ml) **cane sugar–based ginger beer**

2 to 3 drops **black walnut bitters**

Add all the liquid ingredients except the ginger beer and bitters to a tall mixing glass with a few hand-cut cubes of ice. Stir to chill and combine. Then, place a cube or two of hand-cut ice into each of two Collins glasses. Strain the mixture over the ice, and drip the black walnut bitters over the top of each drink. Add two tall straws, and you're done. Serves two woeful drinkers. Plan accordingly.

Scotch Whisky

Ah, Scotch. The very word is enough to send waves

of warmth through your body, and to revive flagging spirits on a cold winter's day, and I'll bet it brings back a whole host of memories, too. Maybe your dad or your grandfather used to sip a neat Scotch as a nightcap every evening before bed. Perhaps your mom had a top-secret recipe for frozen Scotch sours—all tart and sweet, dotted with cocktail cherries—that she'd whip up for company on a long summer's evening. Then again, maybe your memories of Scotch are of your own experimentations: like the time, as a sweet-toothed twenty-two-year-old, that you poured it over vanilla ice cream and gasped at the way the hot, smoky liquid blended with the ice cream's cold, luscious sweetness, or when your college professor opened a bottle of single-malt on the sly in his office and shared a drop of neat *aqua vitae* with a couple lucky students.

The amber liquid certainly looms large in the collective memory of drinkers around the world, and whether you're an expert or a neophyte when it comes to Scotch, I'll wager you're familiar with the tipple, if only in theory. So, what is the stuff, anyway? Basically, "Scotch" refers to malt whisky or grain whisky (note the spelling: There's no "I" in "team," but in Scotland, there's no "e" in "whisky," either) that's made in Scotland. (By law, whiskies labeled as "Scotch" must be made in Scotland, so don't bother looking: You won't find American-made Scotch.) It's often made from barley, which has been malted. That is, the grains have been placed in water and allowed to germinate, and are then removed from the water and dried in hot air to stop the germination process. Scotch whisky usually clocks in at between forty percent and forty-six percent alcohol by volume, and it must be aged for at least three years (and it's often aged for much longer than that). Part of the aging process often takes place in wooden casks that were formerly used to store port, sherry, or even bourbon.

And Scotch certainly has an estimable history. The first written record of Scotch whisky appeared in the Exchequer Rolls of Scotland in the late fifteenth century, when the king gave enough malt to a Tironesian friar—who was probably also an apothecary—to distill the equivalent of nearly 1,500 bottles of whisky in today's measurements. Clearly, distilling had already been well established in Scotland by this point, so it's safe to say that Scotch whisky is at least many hundreds, if not thousands, of years old. After all, Scotland's landscape has a raw, desolate kind of beauty, and rainy Caledonian weather is par for the course, so it's no wonder that Scotch is so effective in warming the body—its heat filters down to the very soles of your feet—and the soul. (I've often wondered why the climates with the most debilitating weather seem to inspire the production of the most enlightening liquors! Necessity is the mother of invention, I suppose.)

When it comes to the flavor, character, and aromatics of this venerable spirit, each version is unique: Part of the wonder inherent in experimenting with Scotch is that each expression of the spirit will be different from the last one that you tried. Some Scotch whiskies are sweet and delicate; some are lightly smoky and fruity; and some are dark, heavily smoky, peaty, and earthy. Not every variety of Scotch whisky will appeal to you, and that's fine. A good rule of thumb is simply to experiment with an open mind—you're sure to find at least one, if not many, that you enjoy. As in love, so in spirits: Just like the best relationships, knowing and loving Scotch is a quest that can and should become a lifelong endeavor.

But "neat" or "on the rocks" are by no means the only ways to sip Scotch whisky. It's surprisingly versatile and can be used as the base for scores of fabulous cocktails. And I don't mean simply adding a dash of soda water and a couple of ice cubes; you'll be astounded at the variety of flavors that complement Scotch. The drinks in this chapter prove it. If a savory tipple is your style, a Moors at Night Punch is your only man: It's a sturdy beef broth infused with fresh herbs, topped up with a healthy helping of Scotch and some fresh lemon juice that's sure to put a lift in your step. Scotch is a wonderful match for fruit, too. If you want proof, just try a Thoreau Cocktail with Warm Cranberry, Blueberry, and Scotch. One of my favorite short drinks is the Old Ships of Battle, a twisted version of the classic Rob Roy: It substitutes a cherry liqueuer called Cherry Heering for the sweet vermouth, among other amendments. And, although it doesn't sound likely, Scotch can easily be paired with tropical ingredients, as in the Another Thor Cocktail, where it meets fresh citrus juices, coconut, orgeat syrup, and club soda.

Keep reading: Your love affair with Scotch starts now.

Note to the Reader:

All recipes make a single serving,
unless otherwise indicated.

Moors at Night Punch

Scotch is the essential ingredient in many hot punches, and with good reason: There's really no better restorative for both body and soul. Scotch works its healing magic not only through its soothing-yet-stimulating smoky taste but also through its scent; a mere sniff of a hot, Scotch-based cocktail is enough to calm the nerves and warm the bones. If you've been roaming England's chilly moors with a heavy tread (or if you just feel like you have), rest assured that this savory potion will help you beat the "brrr." Combining steaming-hot, herb-infused beef bouillon with a hearty dose of Scotch and a whack of fresh lemon juice, the Moors at Night Punch was inspired by a couple of particularly cold winters I spent on Midcoast Maine during the 1980s.

1 cup (235 ml) **very hot, strong beef bouillon**

Assorted herbs from the garden, such as thyme, rosemary, sage, and lavender

1 **cheesecloth bag** for steeping the herbs

3 ounces (90 ml) **smoky Scotch whisky**

2 tablespoons (30 ml) **Raw Honey Simple Syrup (see page 157)**

1 ounce (30 ml) **freshly squeezed lemon juice (no scurvy aboard this ship!)**

Prepare the bouillon in a small saucepan. Place the herbs in a cheesecloth bag, and steep them in the hot bouillon for about five minutes. Preheat a ceramic mug by pouring boiling water into it, and then pour the water out. Add the whisky and Raw Honey Simple Syrup to the mug, and then pour the herb-steeped bouillon over the mixture. Finally, stir in the fresh lemon juice. Serves two frozen souls.

Thoreau Cocktail with
Warm Cranberry, Blueberry, and Scotch

While the original Thoreau Cocktail calls for botanical gin, I find that Scotch, due to its depth of flavor, is an even better pairing for cranberries and blueberries. If at all possible, use wild Maine blueberries to mix up my Cocktail Whisperer's twisted take on the Thoreau. Wild Maine blueberries bear little resemblance to the run-of-the-mill, plump-and-juicy berries you find in the supermarket: They're tiny, about the size of your fingernail or even smaller, with an intense taste and great acidity. I think they're an excellent match for tart New England cranberries in lots of cocktails, and this Thoreau is one of my favorites. Go ahead and use an inexpensive Scotch here: The crushed fruit and fresh citrus juice would mask the advantages of a pricey one. Oh, and not that you need another excuse to use blueberries in your cocktails, but just in case: Blueberries are reputed to be "superfoods," packed with disease-fighting antioxidants.

¼ cup (35 g) **each crushed cranberries and blueberries**

⅓ cup (85 g) **unsweetened, smooth cranberry sauce (with a bit of sugar added for taste)**

4 ounces (120 ml) **blended Scotch whisky (no single malts in this one!)**

⅓ cup (80 ml) **water**

1 cup (235 ml) **cranberry juice**

¼ cup (60 ml) **freshly squeezed lime juice**

1 tablespoon (15 ml) **maple syrup (optional)**

Several thickly cut orange slices

2 sprigs **of fresh thyme**

Using a muddler or the end of a wooden spoon, muddle the crushed cranberries with the blueberries in the bottom of a heatproof mixing glass to make a slurry, and then add the cranberry sauce to the mix. Add the Scotch, and let sit for a few minutes so the flavors combine. In a small saucepan, bring the water to the boil, and then add the cranberry and lime juices. Pour this heated cranberry juice over the muddled cranberry-blueberry mixture, and stir together. Divide between 2 preheated ceramic mugs, straining the cooked fruit out first, if you like. Sweeten with the maple syrup (if using), and garnish each mug with the orange slices and a sprig of thyme.

The Robert Burns Cocktail

Scotch whisky is an essential ingredient in the Robert Burns cocktail, a tipple that honors Scotland's most famous poet. (Some drinkers think that this classic cocktail was named after a cigar salesman of the same name, but I prefer the literary association. So there!) Every sip of the Robbie Burns is pure elegance, whether it's served straight up in a martini glass with a flamed orange zest twist, or over a crystal-clear chunk of hand-cut ice. That said, if you're a "wee tim'rous beastie," as Burns himself wrote, steer clear: This cocktail is not for the faint of heart. If you can handle it, though, it's a truly luxurious way to start an evening. Try it as an aperitif alongside a handful of spiced cashews, or with a sweet-and-smoky *hors d'oeuvre*, like bacon-wrapped dates.

2 ounces (60 ml) **Scotch whisky**

¾ ounce (22 ml) **Italian vermouth, such as Carpano Antica**

Dash of orange bitters

Dash of absinthe

Orange zest twist (optional)

Fill a cocktail shaker three-quarters full with ice. Pour all the liquid ingredients over the ice. Using a long-handled bar spoon, stir gently to combine. Strain this into a martini glass. Singe the orange zest twist by holding it firmly behind a lit match and pinching it to release its natural citrus oils. (Be careful to spritz the citrus oils into the glass.) Or, pour the mixture over a large chunk of hand-cut ice in a rocks glass, serve, and lift your glass to auld Scotland.

Old Ships of Battle

You've met and loved the classic Rob Roy; now drink this. Old Ships of Battle is my Cocktail Whisperer's twisted take on the Scottish legend. It replaces the sweet vermouth with the old-fashioned cherry liqueur known as Cherry Heering. (First produced in the early nineteenth century, Cherry Heering is a spiced, cherry-based liqueur that isn't terribly sweet, and it's also used in drinks like the Singapore Sling. On the off chance you can't find it, try cherry brandy instead.) Then it calls for a whack of dry vermouth. Instead of plain old Angostura bitters, it kicks things up with a dash or three of strangely beguiling lemon bitters for a citrusy, aromatic finish. In a shout-out to the great British age of sail, I've named this drink Old Ships of Battle, and I think it's best enjoyed before lunch on a blustery spring day.

2 ounces (60 ml) **blended Scotch whisky**

½ ounce (15 ml) **Cherry Heering**

½ ounce (15 ml) **dry vermouth**

Several shakes of lemon bitters

Club soda

Fill a Collins glass with a couple hand-cut ice cubes. Add the Scotch, Cherry Heering, and the dry vermouth. Stir with a bar spoon. Add the lemon bitters, and top with club soda. Sip, and while you're at it, toast the iron-sided ships and the ironmen who sailed them.

The Thomas Riley Marshall Cocktail

Depending on its *terroir*, Scotch whisky can taste richly earthy and spicy, followed by a long, vanilla-flavored finish. Named for the U.S. vice president who said, infamously (and, one hopes, with his tongue firmly in his cheek), "What this country needs is a really good five-cent cigar," the Thomas Riley Marshall cocktail can really make Scotch sing. Here, peach brandy lends a layer of juicy, freshly crushed peaches that brings out Scotch's spicy sweetness, plus a wisp of woody vanilla, where the brandy kissed the oak cask in which it was confined. A final touch of curried bitters adds depth and more spice. The Thomas Riley Marshall features only a few ingredients, but its simplicity belies its depth—you'll be enchanted by its spicy, sweet heat.

2 ounces (60 ml) **blended Scotch whiskey**

¼ ounce (7 ml) **peach brandy**

Several drops of curried bitters

Easy Home-Cured Cocktail Cherries (see page 156)

Pre-chill a rocks glass by filling it with ice water, and then pour the ice water out. Wash the inside of the glass with the peach brandy, and then pour the brandy out (into your mouth, please—what have I told you about wasting good liquor?) Add a single hand-cut ice cube to the glass, followed by the Scotch. Dribble 2 to 4 drops of the curried bitters over the top of the drink, and garnish with an Easy Home-Cured Cocktail Cherry. Then light up that imaginary five-cent cigar, and kick back for the evening.

The Classic Rob Roy Cocktail

My grandfather was very fond of a pre-dinner Rob Roy. For him, there was no better way to stimulate the appetite and to relax before a family meal. Well, times change, but the effects of good Scotch don't, and this cocktail is as delicious as it was when it was first created in the late nineteenth century in New York City. A kissing cousin of the Manhattan—the Manhattan calls for rye whiskey, where the Rob Roy employs Scotch—this drink is named after the eighteenth-century Scottish hero Rob Roy MacGregor, and it's as noble as its namesake. Here's the time-honored recipe. It's exactly how my grandfather enjoyed them back in the day, and it'll be just as popular a hundred years from now.

3 ounces (90 ml) **blended Scotch whisky**

½ ounce (15 ml) **sweet vermouth**

Angostura bitters

....

Chill a Martini glass until frosty by filling it with ice water, and then pour the ice water out. Shake a dash or two of the Angostura bitters into the martini glass. Then, fill a cocktail mixing glass three-quarters full with ice. Add the Scotch and the sweet vermouth. Stir and strain into the pre-chilled, bitters-drizzled martini glass. Serve immediately—then get to work preparing a second round.

Belle Isle Cocktail

Brewing up a strong hot toddy is one of my favorite ways to get rid of a headache or to put the kibosh on a pesky cold. And Scotch makes a top-notch toddy: Combining Scotch with hot water or strong black tea enhances its peaty flavor. (I prefer tea, to be honest, since watery toddies aren't up my alley; but if you're avoiding caffeine, hot water really does work just as well. Or, you might try decaffeinated black tea instead.) Scotch, fresh lemon juice, hot black tea, and simple syrup combine in the Belle Isle Cocktail for a hot punch that really packs a punch. This gorgeous little glug comprises no more than four simple ingredients, but it's certain to help you shake that woolly-headedness that accompanies winter colds and other bugs. Apply as needed.

2 ounces (60 ml) **Scotch whisky**

1 ounce (30 ml) **Basic Simple Syrup (see page 156)**

3 ounces (90 ml) **freshly brewed strong black tea**

1 ounce (30 ml) **freshly squeezed lemon juice**

Preheat your favorite ceramic mug by filling it with boiling water, and then pour the water out. Add the simple syrup and the Scotch to the mug, followed by the tea and the fresh lemon juice. Stir gently. Serve and sip, preferably under a warm quilt.

Sailor's Dilemma

It's widely held that a hot cup of strong, meaty broth mixed with a robust Scotch whisky is far greater than the sum of its parts. And it's true. The Sailor's Dilemma is a simple combination of the two—but the results, when you're feeling under the weather, are pretty close to magical. The broth, for its part, heals you deeply; what the Scotch does is anyone's guess! But seriously, folks, this really is a hearty restorative. The whisky will relax you a bit, so that you can get a bit of much-needed shuteye, and hot liquids help ease chest and sinus congestion. By the way, I know it's tempting to use a bouillon cube if you haven't got the real thing on hand, but do try to avoid them—homemade broth is a far better accompaniment to your precious Scotch.

8 ounces (235 ml) **hot, strong beef, lamb, or chicken broth**

3 ounces (90 ml) **Scotch whisky**

Pre-heat your mug by filling it with boiling water, and then pour the water out. Add the Scotch to the mug, and top with the strong broth. Job done. Now, sip slowly, dreaming of sunnier climes. Serves two sailors.

Another Thor Cocktail

You might not think that Scotch is a match for Tiki-style drinks, with their fresh citrus juices and coconutty sweetness—but now is the time to think again. The saline, smoky finish of, say, an Islay Scotch whisky makes it just as desirable in tropical cocktails as hearty, barrel-aged rum. Named for the Norse god of thunder, Another Thor mixes good Islay Scotch with orange, pineapple, lemon, and lime juices, as well as a little orgeat syrup (orgeat is a sweet, almond-flavored syrup that's used in lots of cocktails, such as the Mai Tai). A dash of curried bitters and a splash of palate-lifting club soda make for a surprising finish to this sultry summery cocktail. It's just the thing for sipping poolside—or, if you're on vacation, at brunch.

2 ounces (60 ml) **Islay-style Scotch whisky**

1 ounce (30 ml) **freshly squeezed orange juice**

1 ounce (30 ml) **freshly squeezed pineapple juice**

¼ ounce (7 ml) **freshly squeezed lemon juice**

¼ ounce (7 ml) **freshly squeezed lime juice**

1 ounce (30 ml) **sweetened coconut cream (sweetened)**

½ ounce (15 ml) **orgeat**

Splash of club soda

3 drops **curried bitters**

Fill a Boston shaker three-quarters full with ice. Add all the ingredients except the club soda and the bitters. Shake for about 15 seconds. Strain the mixture over a single hand-cut ice cube in a rocks glass. Add the splash of club soda, and drip the curried bitters over the top of the drink. Serve, wearing a grass skirt.

Whiskeys Around the Globe

When you think of the word "whiskey," I bet a whole host of images come to mind. Perhaps your thoughts drift toward Kentucky's famous bluegrass and to the gentle twanging of banjos. Maybe you meditate upon the heather-swathed fields of the Scottish countryside—or on Glasgow's grey streets, or on the lofty heights of Edinburgh Castle. Do you ruminate upon the backwoods distillers of Tennessee, who brewed their moonshine in backyard stills, even during Prohibition? Get ready to take your thoughts—and your palate—even further afield. There's great whiskey to be found elsewhere in the world, in places like Ireland (no surprise there), France (nope, it's not the same thing as cognac), Japan, and India. And that's not all: Did you know that Taiwan, South Africa, and Australia, for example, all produce excellent, award-winning whiskeys as well? Whiskey's ancestral home may be Scotland, but today, the spirit is a true globetrotter.

Let's start with the Emerald Isle. Not too long ago, I saw a guy wearing a bright-green t-shirt that read, "Irish whiskey makes me frisky." It's a sentiment I agree with, at least in part: The mere thought of the changing landscape of Irish whiskey is enough to perk up my taste buds. Unlike the whisky produced by Ireland's neighbor from just across the pond (that's Scotland, for the geographically challenged), Irish whiskey hasn't got that smokiness that's so characteristic of Scotch. It does its own thing: Some of the best Irish whiskeys are redolent of spice, maple syrup, butterscotch, and toasted nuts, and they're lovely in scores of cocktails.

When it comes to French tipples, grape-based products are the best known, of course: think Bordeaux wine, Champagne, or Cognac and Armagnac. But luxurious, soft French whisky (note that missing "e") is right up there with the best in the world. It's more similar to Scotch whisky than its Irish counterpart, but it's decidedly sweeter, with a flavor profile that can smack of light smoke and sea salt. Where Scotch can be quite robust in the mouth, though, French whisky is lush and silky smooth on the tongue, thanks to the use of the French-oak barrels that were once used to store cognac.

Like French whisky, Japanese whisky's closest cousin is Scotch. That said, it's decidedly lighter than Scotch whisky, with fine strands of smoke woven through its flavor profile like the whisper of fine silk. You can expect more salt and smoke on the nose and palate than French whisky—thanks to sweet, slowly cooked long grains that seem to be mixed with a tangle of iodiney seaweed. When it comes to mixology, it's easy to use Japanese whisky in cocktails, since it can act as a foil to stronger ingredients.

If you travel southwest from Japan, you'll run smack into the home of one of the biggest trends in whiskey production. South Asia is hot for whiskey at the moment, and you might be surprised to learn that the Indian whisky market is the third largest in the world, falling just behind China and Russia. Remember, lots of Indian "whiskies" aren't made with grain at all but use sugarcane and caramel coloring and flavoring to tempt the uninitiated. (Sugarcane? That's not whisky—that's rum!) Steer well clear of the stuff, unless you want to earn yourself a legendary hangover. Now, that's not to say that top-quality, malted-grain-based whiskeys aren't being distilled in India—they sure are. It's just that there's only so much malted grain available in India, and what is available doesn't come cheap.

Then there's the hot, humid climate to contend with: During the aging process, up to half of a barrel of Indian whisky can evaporate into thin air due to the high temperatures. This means that true Indian can be pricey—but the country is turning out some great examples of single-malt Scotch-style whisky

that are winning accolades at international competitions. More and more drinkers are discovering the beguiling nature of this über–high-end product. Thirsty yet? I know I am. In this chapter, I'll show you lots of ways to work whiskeys from around the world into your mixological repertoire. You can't go wrong with my ever-so-slightly twisted take on the classic Café Irlandés, aka Irish coffee. If you think it's as ho-hum as chucking some Bushmill's into a cup of joe, think again: My version uses absinthe, hand-whipped cream, and dark-brown sugar for a hot, decadent treat that's great for sipping after dinner or on a dusky winter's afternoon. If you're feeling French, mix up Le James Brown cocktail, an iced take on the Irlandés—here, French whiskey meets iced espresso, whipped cream, club soda, and fragrant, freshly grated nutmeg. Or, mix Japanese whisky with *sake,* plus a pinch of sea salt and a cucumber slice, for a minimalist cocktail that's sure to bring out the Zen in you. You'll also learn how to match Indian whisky with absinthe, simple syrup, and fizzy water for a Southeastern take on the Scotch-and-soda—and how to mix up a pitcher of summer, otherwise known as the David Balfour cocktail: It's proof that Irish whiskey is a perfect partner for fresh lemonade spiked with mint.

Read on, and you'll see just how international the whiskey phenomenon is.

Note to the Reader:

All recipes make a single serving,
unless otherwise indicated.

Sunset Over The Ganges Cocktail

This exotic cocktail is sure to whet your appetite, wet your whistle, and cool your brow on a sultry summer's evening. And ice is the major consideration here, so please make your coconut water ice the day before—or at least eight hours before—you plan to enjoy one of these. The ice must be perfectly firm so that it can be shaved properly. How does one shave ice, you ask? Buy or borrow a woodworker's rasp (if you decide to do the latter, please remove all wood splinters, oils, et cetera, before you attempt to shave the ice!). The consistency you're going for is a sort of a fine, slushy, coconutty gravel. Combined with whisky and a dash of spice from Teapot Bitters, this mysterious combination of South Asian ingredients mimics India's sweet-and-spicy chai tea. Remember, don't use the cheap stuff: Use only a high-quality brand of single-malt Indian whisky for this cocktail.

3 ounces (90 ml) **Indian whisky**

1 ounce (30 ml) **Basic Simple Syrup (see page 156)**

Shaved ice, made from coconut water

½ ounce (15 ml) **club soda**

5 drops **Teapot Bitters**

Shave the coconut water ice with a woodworking rasp (if it's not brand-new, make sure it's absolutely clean of any wood shavings or oils). The ice should be the consistency of the Italian ices you loved as a kid. Keep the coconut water ice dry by placing a dry cloth over it. Fill a mixing glass three-quarters full with plain ice. Add the whisky and the simple syrup. Stir well until chilled. Pack an old-fashioned glass with the shaved coconut water ice, and strain the mixture on top of the shaved ice. Top with the club soda, and drip 5 drops of the Teapot Bitters over the top of the drink. Garnish with two small bar straws. Sip, and watch the sun go down.

Café Irlandés

This exotic hot drink is a layered cocktail, based on the *pousse-café*, a cocktail in which several different kinds of liquor are carefully layered on top of one another. Where the *pousse-café* is served cold, however, the Café Irlandés is served piping hot. It's a combination of strong, hot coffee; sweet, thick whipped cream; and perky, spicy Irish whiskey. And it's impossible to make without softly made, hand-whipped cream. (Whatever you do, never use that stuff that comes in a can.) The kind of whipped cream that makes this drink sing is more like a thickly textured emulsion that sticks to the sides of the glass when poured. The result is a magical concoction that's *digestif* and dessert all in one. Try not to have more than two: Otherwise, you'll be caught in a tug-of-war between the caffeine and the alcohol.

2 tablespoons (30 g) **dark brown sugar**

3 ounces (90 ml) **espresso coffee**

3 ounces (90 ml) **Irish whiskey**

2 ounces (60 ml) **hand-whipped cream**

¼ ounce (7 ml) **absinthe**

Preheat a strong wineglass or latte-style coffee glass by filling it with boiling water, and then pour the water out. Add the sugar and about a third of the coffee, and stir with a bar spoon. Then add about a third of the whiskey, by pouring it over the back of a dessert spoon into the glass. Then spoon some cream into the glass, followed by a bit more sugar, and a bit more whiskey. Repeat the process until you've used up all whiskey, sugar, and coffee. (Work slowly; it's an art form, not a race!) Finally, using a medicine dropper, drip the absinthe over the top of the cocktail. Sláinte!

David Balfour Cocktail

Named for the resourceful protagonist of Robert Louis Stevenson's novel *Kidnapped,* this refreshing tipple is just as enterprising. Its simple ingredients make it easy to prepare in a flash, and they also travel well in a go-cup, if you want to save your portion of David Balfour for later on. Make your own lemonade with freshly squeezed lemon juice, some cool spring water, simple syrup, and some torn fresh mint—then zest it up with orange bitters and a healthy pour of Irish whiskey. (I recommend trying a few different varieties of orange bitters before you settle on one that really resonates with you: There are lots of versions available on the market.) Mix up a jug of David B. to take with you on your next picnic, barbeque, or trip to the beach: It goes wonderfully with just about all lunchtime noshes.

8 ounces (235 ml) **Irish whiskey**

10 ounces (285 ml) **fresh lemonade, sweetened to taste with Basic Simple Syrup (see page 156)**

1 small bunch **fresh mint, washed well and torn or slapped**

4 shakes **orange bitters**

Fill a pitcher three-quarters full with ice. Add the slapped or torn mint, followed by the Irish whiskey and the sweetened lemonade. Mix gently. Shake the orange bitters over the top—taste for balance, adding more bitters if necessary. Serves four picnickers.

North Atlantic Capital Cocktail

I am pleased to introduce you to an Irish legend. Meet *poitín,* a word that means "little pot" in Irish. Pronounced "PUTCH-een," the stuff flies under the radar in the land of Forty Shades. This Irish moonshine is distilled from a mash that consists of things like barley, potatoes, and even whey. It's almost impossible to drink poitín straight, since its alcohol levels can approach 190 proof. A miniscule bottle of only 50 milliliters is capable of completely obliterating both the body and the mind of a grown man. So watch out for this raucous tipple, and use it sparingly. Can't find the real thing? No worries: Try making a North Atlantic Capital with your favorite white whiskey instead.

¼ ounce (7 ml) **poitín or white whiskey**

¼ ounce (7 ml) **each freshly squeezed nectarine, lemon, and orange juices**

2 ounces (60 ml) **club soda**

Aromatic bitters

Pinch of sea salt

Fill a mixing glass three-quarters full with ice. Add the poitín and the fruit juices, stir gently, and strain into a small glass. Top with the club soda, dot with the aromatic bitters, and sprinkle a pinch of sea salt over the top of the drink for a subtle, saline crunch. You won't need more than one. Seriously.

A Sensible Thing

A Sensible Thing, with its whisky and freshly squeezed lemon juice for snap and acidity, is a bit of an oxymoron: a chilled toddy. Like a hot toddy, though, it's still a wonderful way to revive body and soul. I like to twist my toddy up a bit by adding yuzu syrup (yuzu is a Japanese citrus fruit) and a final float of plum wine. I finish it off with a bit of fizzy water for lift, and I always serve it over a hand-cut-and-polished ice round. A Sensible Thing is fabulously refreshing, but observe the name and sip 'em sensibly—more than a couple, and you might find your faculties seriously compromised.

1 ounce (28 g) **chopped pickled ginger**

1 ounce (30 ml) **yuzu syrup (store-bought, or make your own Orange Simple Syrup: see page 157)**

1 ounce (30 ml) **lemon juice**

2 ounces (60 ml) **Japanese whisky**

¼ ounce (7 ml) **plum wine**

Using a muddler or the end of a wooden spoon, muddle the pickled ginger in a mixing glass. Add the yuzu citrus syrup and the lemon juice. Then, fill the mixing glass three-quarters full with ice. Add the whisky, and mix carefully with a bar spoon. Using a Hawthorne strainer, strain the mixture over a single hand-cut ice cube into a coupé glass. Float the plum wine over the top of the drink, and sip—sensibly, of course.

The Fleming Jenkins Fizz

The Fleming Jenkins Fizz is a variation on the *ti'punch* theme. Ferocious *ti'punch* has its origins in the Caribbean islands like Martinique, Guadeloupe, and Haiti, where *rhum agricole* was traditionally mixed with sugar-cane syrup and fresh lime juice for an aperitif that's so potent, it'd knock more than just your socks off. I think Indian whisky, with its denser mouth feel, is really intriguing when it's mixed with homemade simple syrup, absinthe, and club soda, and it makes a smashing aperitif or an accompaniment to a light, summery lunch like a salad of baby spinach, fresh mango, grilled chicken, sweet potato crisps, and cashew nuts. Don't wait for warm weather to treat yourself to a Fleming Jenkins, though: All you need on hand is a good bottle of Indian whisky. The rest is easy.

2 ounces (60 ml) **Indian "Scotch-style" whisky**

1 ounce (30 ml) **cane-sugar syrup (or Basic Simple Syrup: see page 156)**

¼ ounce (7 ml) **absinthe**

Splash of club soda

Curried bitters

Fill a cocktail shaker three-quarters full with ice. Add the syrup, absinthe, and the Indian whisky. Shake well for about 20 seconds, and strain over one cube of hand-cut ice into a rocks glass. Add a splash of club soda and three drops of curried bitters, and serve immediately. Then start preparing round two!

Le James Brown Cocktail

There's no better way to finish off a great dinner party than with a round of Le James Browns. It's an elegant riff on the Irish coffee, and since it's served chilled, it's perfect for summer evenings when you're dying for a *digestif* but can't stand the thought of hot liquids. In it, French whisky meets chilled espresso, black walnut bitters, a dash of club soda, and a dollop of easy-to-make, cognac-spiked whipped cream—along with a little freshly grated nutmeg for good measure. (Feel free to prepare the espresso well in advance—even the day before is fine.) Serve it alongside (or after) a simple, light dessert, like fresh berries over cognac-laced vanilla ice cream—or, with a few good shortbread cookies.

4 ounces (120 ml) **chilled espresso coffee**

2 ounces (60 ml) **French whisky**

Splash of club soda

½ cup (115 g) **Cognac Whipped Cream (see page 156)**

Scraping of fresh nutmeg

8 drops **Black Walnut bitters**

Brew your espresso and let it cool either in an ice bath or overnight in the fridge. Add several large cubes of ice to each of two Collins glasses. Top each with 1 ounce (30 ml) of the chilled espresso in each glass, followed by the French whisky. Splash a bit of club soda on top of each drink, then spoon the sweetened, thick cream over the mixture. Scrape a little fresh nutmeg over the top of each glass, and finish each with 4 drops of bitters. Serves two thirsty heads. In the immortal words of Brown himself: You'll feel good!

Leaves Straining Against Wind

Picture this: It's late autumn. The trees are nearly barren of leaves, and a single leaf hangs onto its branch by sheer willpower, despite the chill winds. You gaze up at the tenacious leaf and meditate upon the past, the possibilities the future holds, and the truth inherent in the present moment. Then you take a sip of this exquisite slurp— and while you might not reach immediate enlightenment, the stuff in your glass sure tastes good. A drink to be enjoyed oh-so-slowly, Leaves Straining Against Wind comprises no more than four ingredients: Japanese whisky, enriched by a splash of savory *junmai sake,* plus some fizzy, salty club soda and a paper-thin slice of cucumber. No need for ice here: For this cocktail, cool cellar temperatures are best. Serve it in your favorite teacup.

2 ounces (60 ml) **high-quality Japanese whisky**

½ ounce (15 ml) **high-quality *junmai sake***

Thinly cut cucumber slices

Pinch of sea salt

Add a pinch of sea salt to a mid-sized ceramic tea cup. Pop a cube of hand-cut ice into the cup, and then pour the whisky over it. Float the sake on top of the whiskey, and garnish with a cucumber slice. Sip slowly and meditatively.

José Gaspar Cocktail

Each year, Tampa, Florida holds the Gasparilla Pirate Festival. It's named for the Spanish pirate José Gaspar, who was, at first, a perfectly gentlemanly buccaneer, licensed by the Spanish crown to make a living by preying on merchant ships in the Gulf of Mexico and the Caribbean. However, legend has it, he went rogue and attacked Tampa. He came to no good end. This fruity, liquor-laden libation is an unlikely combination of two rogue spirits: Irish whiskey and rum, and this combination of the two best-known sea-going liquors has been known to transform the living into the living dead. (Metaphorically of course.)

2 ounce (60 ml) **Irish whiskey**

1 ounce (30 ml) **dark rum**

½ ounce (15 ml) **pineapple juice**

½ ounce (15 ml) **orange juice**

½ ounce (15 ml) **grapefruit juice**

¼ ounce (7 ml) *crème de banane*

½ ounce (15 ml) **Homemade Grenadine Syrup (see page 156)**

4 drops **curried bitters (use your favorite brand or make your own: see page 156)**

Fill a mixing glass three-quarters full with ice. Add all the ingredients except the bitters, and mix well to chill. Strain the mixture into a parfait glass half-filled with crushed ice. To finish, drip the curried bitters over the top of each drink. Serves two landlubbers out at sea for the first time.

Dr. Somerset's Cure

In Robert Louis Stevenson's short story *The Superfluous Mansion*, one character inquires of another, "'Have you a drop of Brandy… I am sick.'" Back in the day, brandy was thought to be medicinal and a restorative—so if you needed an excuse to treat yourself to a brandy-laced cocktail, look no further. Dr. Somerset's Cure features both brandy and French whisky, which is often aged in casks that once held cognac. The result is a softly oaked spirit that's truly the stuff of dreams.

5 to 6 **Roasted Apricots (see Roasted Stone Fruits, page 157)**

1 ounce (30 ml) **sweet vermouth**

1 ounce (30 ml) **French whisky**

½ ounce (15 ml) **calvados**

2 **orange segments (remove as much of the white pith as possible)**

1 ounce (30 ml) **lemon juice**

1 ounce (30 ml) **Raw Honey Simple Syrup (see page 157)**

2 to 3 shakes **pimento bitters**

Add 3 roasted apricot halves to a Boston shaker, and pour the vermouth over them. Using a muddler or the end of a wooden spoon, muddle the apricot with the vermouth. Then, add the French whisky and the calvados, and continue muddling, adding the orange segments, the lemon juice, and the Raw Honey Simple Syrup in turns. When well combined, divide the mixture between four rocks glasses with one cube of ice cube in each, and finish with a dash or two of the pimento bitters over the top of each glass. Serves 4.

Cooking with Whiskey

To borrow shamelessly again from the Bard: To cook with whiskey, or not to cook with whiskey? That's the question. Some purists blanch at the thought of throwing away their precious single-malt in cooking: Why waste expensive whiskey, they'd argue, by using it as an ingredient? Especially since, in recipes that involve applying any kind of heat at all, the alcohol will inevitably evaporate? Isn't that the same thing as pouring it down the drain?

Certainly not: In the kitchen—regardless of which dish you're preparing—the finished product is only as good as the sum of its parts. So it makes sense to use the best-quality stuff you can afford. Don't get me wrong: If you're not a Silicon Valley millionaire, I'm not suggesting you blow big bucks on a pricey whiskey—either for sipping, or for using in recipes. Just like wine (and beer, and lots of other spirits, for that matter), a halfway decent whiskey makes a marvelous addition to, quite literally, thousands of recipes. That's because whiskey is such a versatile ingredient. It seems to bring out the essence of whatever you happen to be making, whether that something is sweet of savory. It makes a cracking fish cure and a marvelous steak marinade. It's magnificent with raw oysters, and, of course, with smoked fish like salmon or mackerel. (It's even great with sushi.) In parts of the United Kingdom, it's an essential ingredient in Christmas cakes and wedding cakes.

Lots of cooks add it to condiments like chutney, or better yet, orange marmalade: It's just the thing for spreading on freshly cut, buttered, toasted bread and enjoying alongside a strong cup of tea. If the word "flambé" appears in the recipe directions, reach for a bottle of whiskey instead of cognac: It'll work just as well. When it comes to the sweet stuff, whiskey adds depth and "kick" to vanilla-flavored desserts, and it warms up just about anything involving chocolate, from brownies to luscious, pourable chocolate sauces. And, like wine, whiskey can be paired with cheeses of just about every description.

That's not all. Whiskey, with its complex flavors and aromatics, matches well with a wide variety of herbs and spices. Think wintery flavors like ginger, aniseed, cinnamon, and allspice—but not to the exclusion of fresh herbs like peppery basil, sharp, fresh mint, savory thyme, and aniseed-esque tarragon. And—as you've probably already noticed, from many of the cocktails in this book—it's delicious with anything citrusy.

So, we've established that you can and should cook with whiskey. What about drinking it alongside food? We're all used to drinking wine or beer with meals, but lots of us tend to restrict our whiskey to one or two before dinner. Then, as soon as the food is served, we put away our Collins or old-fashioned glasses and break out our wine glasses. Fair enough. After all, *vino* and *biere* were made to be accompanied by food. But so is whiskey. The flavors and aromatics of whiskeys are, arguably, even more diverse than those of wine. So there's no reason you shouldn't enjoy your favorite whiskey (or whisky)—served neat or as the main ingredient in a cocktail—while you're relishing a good meal.

What's the answer to our conundrum, then? Is it best to drink whiskey, or to cook with it? Do both, of course. Thus far, you've learned dozens of new ways to enjoy whiskey, but they've all been served in a glass. Now it's time to take your favorite bottle of whiskey into the kitchen! Here are some of my favorite recipes for this most versatile of spirits.

To make lunchtime spectacular, make up a few Bourbon and Maple Syrup–Glazed Ham and Swiss Sandwiches. Bourbon and pork are a great combination—and when they're paired with Dijon mustard, the result is a sweet-and-savory bite of porcine heaven that's complemented by slices of nutty Swiss cheese. Then, offer your guests a plateful of Oatmeal Raisin Whoopie Pies: They're an all-grown-up version of the chewy treats you loved as a kid. Since both the cream cheese filling and the raisins are soaked in Drambuie (a Scotch-based liqueur whose Scotch-Gaelic name translates as "the drop that satisfies") they have a kick that's a hundred percent adult. And whiskey isn't just for carnivores: The Scotch whisky in my Hearty Barley, Lentil, and Vegetable Stew (which is naturally vegan and gluten-free, by the way) adds a dose of heat and smoky flavor that makes it one of the best winter warmers I know.

There are reams of recipes that use whiskey to make them shine: Read on to discover the best of them.

A Scotsman's Flourish

Feed a cold and starve a fever, the old saying goes. It's true: If you're feeling under the weather, it's even more important to eat regularly and healthfully. Nutritious meals can play a huge part in boosting the immune system. That's where this steaming bowl of classic, steel-cut oatmeal comes in. Spiked with a generous serving of whisky-soaked dried fruit, A Scotsman's Flourish comes at the final stage of this breakfast of champions—you'll top your bowl with an extra ounce or two of Scotch for good measure. It just goes to show that you can eat your breakfast and drink it too! And there's no need to waste any Scotch: Pour the whiskey left over from steeping the dried fruit over another cup of dried cherries in a sterilized container. Refrigerate these gorgeous home-cured cherries for garnishing your Manhattans, or serve them over vanilla gelato for dessert.

Bowl of steel-cut oatmeal, served piping hot

¼ cup (38 g) **dried cherries**

¼ cup (32 g) **dried apricots**

2 ounces (60 ml) **blended Scotch whisky**

½ cup (15 ml) **spring water**

To taste: Raw Honey Simple Syrup (see page 157)

Cook your steel-cut oatmeal for about 45 minutes according to package directions. While it's cooking, add the dried cherries and dried apricots to a glass bowl. Cover with the blended whisky and the water. Let the fruits reconstitute for as long as it takes to cook your oatmeal. Toward the end of cooking, spoon the whisky-softened fruits into the oatmeal, and stir well. Serve in preheated ceramic bowls. Pour the remaining whisky over the top of the oatmeal. Sweeten to taste with Raw Honey Simple Syrup. Then, dig in and enjoy your healing breakfast! For an added kick, serve with a David Balfour Cocktail (see page 134): It'll prove a cool, refreshing contrast to your steaming hot, whisky-laden oatmeal.

Bourbon and Maple Syrup–Glazed Ham and Swiss Sandwiches

Bourbon is one of those ingredients that grooves beautifully against the flavor of a sweet, tangy ham steak. It's so easy to buy a ham these days: Every specialty food catalogue offers the precooked variety. And if you don't want to order one on the web or by mail, visit your local German butcher. Ask him or her for a four- or five-pound ham steak. (If it's not already cured and smoked, get your butcher to do it for you.) Ham steak is a brined, smoked, succulent chunk of porcine heaven. Cut from the pig's leg, it's usually capped with plenty of crackling fat. It makes incredible sandwiches: I like to serve mine on seeded rye bread with a homemade sauce of bourbon and Dijon mustard.

1 ham steak (4 to 5 pounds, or 1.8 to 2.25 kg)

½ cup (15 ml) **bourbon**

½ cup (15 ml) **maple syrup**

2 tablespoons (22 g) **Dijon mustard**

8 slices **seeded rye bread**

4 slices **Swiss cheese**

Grill the ham steak until pronounced grill marks appear on the pinkish meat. Remove from the grill and set aside to cool. Combine the bourbon and maple syrup in a small saucepan. Heat over a very slow flame, in order to burn off most of the alcohol from the bourbon. Your house will be filled with the most incredible aroma as the syrup thickens and reduces. When the glaze is very thick, remove it from the flame and add a few tablespoons of Dijon mustard. Keep warm. Slice the ham steak on a bias. Toast the rye bread and slather with the bourbon mustard glaze. To make each sandwich, place a couple slices of ham on one slice of bread, and drizzle with a little more of the bourbon mustard glaze. Top each with a slice of Swiss cheese, and then place in a toaster oven and broil until the Swiss is nicely melted. Top with another toasted slice of rye, and slice the sandwich in half. Serves 4, with plenty of ham left over for tomorrow's lunch. Serve with a Captain Swank's Sandwich Sippah (see page 74).

Slow-Cooked Suckling Pig
with a Bourbon Barbeque Glaze

If you're a through-and-through carnivore, let my Slow-Cooked Suckling Pig take center stage at your next barbeque. Coated with a toothsome glaze made from bourbon, tomato puree, and raw honey and then slow-cooked until the meat melts in your mouth, this suckling pig makes a great main course for a Fourth of July or Labor Day do. Serve it with everyone's favorite barbeque side dishes, like macaroni salad, potato salad, and corn on the cob. (For dessert, try my Whiskeylicious Oatmeal Raisin Whoopie Pies on page 155!) Remember, when it comes to heat, low and slow is the way to go—don't raise the heat, or the meat will burn and char. You'll just have to be patient: Have another cocktail while you're waiting.

1 **suckling pig** (about 10 to 20 pounds, or 4.5 to 9 kg)

Assorted vegetables of your choice, such as garlic, onion, carrots, celery, and parsnips (choose a nice mélange of flavors, colors and textures)

Assorted dried and fresh herbs of your choice, such as thyme and rosemary

For the glaze:

1 bottle (750 ml) **of bourbon**

2 cans (20 ounces or 570 g) **tomato puree**

2 cups (680 g) **raw honey**

A suckling pig can be roasted in a fire pit over charcoal, on a charcoal grill, or if it's small enough (under 20 pounds, or 9 kg), in your oven. Preheat your oven to 275°F (140°C, or gas mark 1). Season the pig with salt and pepper, and stuff its cavity with the vegetables and herbs. Mix the ingredients for the glaze in a large bowl, and slather the pig with the glaze (glaze the cavity as well). Place the pig in a large roasting pan and cook for about 4 hours (for a 20-pound [9.5-kg] pig: less for a smaller one), basting often with the glaze. To make the skin crispy, turn the heat up to 400°F (200°C, or gas mark 6) for the last 20 to 30 minutes of cooking. Remove the pig from the oven and let it stand for at least 30 minutes before slicing and serving. Serve alongside a bowl of the cooking drippings, so guests can drag each succulent slice through the drippings. Serve with a white whiskey–spiked Bill Monroe's Kentucky Cooler (see page 77).

Bourbon-Laced Turkey Legs and Thighs

Back in the 1980s, I lived in Portland, Maine, and I learned a great deal from working as a line cook at Alberta's Restaurant. After work many of us would pile into a car and find ourselves at Uncle Billy's Barbecue Restaurant, for what I consider to be the best barbeque of my memories. Jonathan St. Laurent was the effusive owner with one foot in Louisiana cooking techniques and the other in France. Sadly, it's closed now, but the sumptuous barbeque served at Uncle Billy's has seasoned my memory to this day. Once, Uncle Billy's nephew Johnny made me a plate of slow-cooked turkey legs and thighs. He bathed them in a combination of tomato sauce, bourbon, brown sugar, and red wine vinegar for nearly twelve hours—and the result was a juicy, aromatic stew, studded with whole shallots and garlic cloves. These Bourbon-Laced Turkey Legs and Thighs are soul food with a French influence, and they're sure to charm you just as wholeheartedly as Johnny's charmed me long ago.

2 **turkey legs and** 2 **turkey thighs, cut into chunks, bone intact**

10 shallots **(no need to peel or smash; just cut off the ends)**

1 bulb **garlic (cut the tops off with a knife, but do not remove the paper)**

1 **Spanish onion, diced**

1 cup (245 g) **marinara sauce**

1 cup (235 ml) **bourbon**

1 cup (200 g) **brown sugar**

1 cup (235 ml) **red wine vinegar**

Preheat your oven to 400°F (200°C, or gas mark 6). Place a cast-iron Dutch oven on the burner over high heat. Season the turkey leg and thigh chunks with salt and pepper. Add some oil to the hot pan and sear the turkey on all sides. Add the shallots, garlic, and onion, and stir. Add the remaining ingredients, place the lid on the Dutch oven, and bake for 30 minutes. Then, reduce the oven temperature to 250°F (120°C, or gas mark ½) and bake for 5 to 6 hours without opening the lid. (Whatever you do, don't open the lid, or the dish will be ruined! Be patient!) Serve with a mess of greens, cooked with a ham bone and a measure of cool spring water to reveal their precious "likker"—that is, the liquid that seeps from the greens when cooking—or with whole tomatoes stewed in oregano, sage and Spanish onions, and sugar. What to drink? Try a lightly fizzy, blueberry-laden Runaway Mountain Train (see page 60).

Roast Turkey
with Bourbon Whiskey Gravy

Bourbon whiskey is the perfect accompaniment to roast turkey's richness. You could just sip a bourbon-centered cocktail alongside your plate of bird, but why not work it right into the recipe? The first thing to do is skip the supermarket. Head straight to your local butcher, and ask him or her for a freshly killed turkey: The difference in taste is incredible. Once you're back home, get stuffing. Fill the cavity with fresh vegetables and fragrant sage before basting the turkey in plenty of bourbon. (Bourbon-soaked drippings make a heavenly gravy, too.) Start early in the day: Large turkeys can take up to 6 hours to roast. It's all worth it, though. Don't wait for Thanksgiving to try this bourbon-soaked roast bird—it's just too good for once a year.

1 **fresh turkey (avoid the frozen variety!)** (20 pounds, or 9 kg)

1 bulb **garlic, with the top sliced off, but without removing the papery skin**

2 whole **shallots**

Assorted fresh vegetables of your choice, such as chopped carrots, celery, parsnips, and turnips

2 **lemons, halved**

2 small bunches **fresh sage**

About 1 cup (30 ml) **bourbon**

Preheat your oven to 400°F (200°C, or gas mark 6). Stuff the turkey's cavity with the garlic, shallots, vegetables, lemons, and half of the sage—then scatter the rest of the sage on and around it. Roast the turkey for 45 minutes, and then turn the heat down to 300°F (150°C, or gas mark 2). Continue to roast for about 6 hours (as a guideline, I usually roast a turkey for 20 minutes per pound, plus a 30-minute resting period after cooking). Baste often with spoonfuls of bourbon and pan drippings. Test the bird during cooking using a good-quality meat thermometer: It should read 165°F (74°C) when done. Remove from the oven, and let stand 30 minutes before carving. Make a delicious gravy by toasting ¼ cup (32 g) flour in a dry pan, and then add a couple tablespoons of softened butter. Add some of the bourbony drippings and enough flour to reach the desired consistency. Serve with a Sleepy Time Down South of Broad (see page 70): A cousin of the mint julep, it acts as a wonderful foil to the juicy turkey.

Williamsburg-Style Mixed Grille

While I was in culinary school, I cooked for a restaurant called the Primerose House in Charleston, South Carolina. There was a lot of freedom in that kitchen, and we cooked with ingredients of the absolute best quality: The fish and other *fruits de mer* were freshly plucked from the sea, still stinging with brackish seawater, while the vegetables were hand-dug each morning from rich black loam, still radiant with morning dew. I'll never forget the Primerose House, and so, thanks to Joann Yaeger, executive chef and founder of the Primerose House and Tavern, I offer you a version of its Williamsburg Mixed Grille. It's a luscious plate of grilled meats, made even more irresistible by my Bourbon Barbeque Dipping Sauce, which also doubles as a glaze.

For the Bourbon Barbeque Dipping Sauce:

1 cup (180 g) **crushed organic tomatoes**	1 **Spanish onion, diced**
1 **stalk celery, diced**	1 **carrot, diced**
1 cup (235 ml) **bourbon**	1 cup (340 g) **raw honey**
2 cloves **finely chopped garlic**	½ **shallot, chopped**
1 teaspoon (5 g) **cayenne pepper (optional)**	

For the mixed grill:

1 **young quail**	1 **baby lamb chop**
1 **dry-aged beef tenderloin** (4 ounces, or 115 g)	
1 **confit-style duck leg**	1 **Boudin sausage**

First, make the dipping sauce. Add all the ingredients to a large sauté pan, and cook on a low heat until the vegetables are soft. Puree the mixture in a food mill, and adjust sweetness with honey to taste. Add the cayenne pepper, if using. To turn the glaze into a tasty dipping sauce, thin with a little extra bourbon. Brush the meats with the glaze, and then grill the assorted meats over charcoal or on a cast-iron griddle. Arrange the meats on a large serving platter, and drizzle a little the bourbon barbeque sauce over the top. Scatter some parsley over the barbeque sauce–covered Williamsburg Mixed Grille and serve sizzling hot, paired with a Classic Rob Roy Cocktail (see page 120).

Fernet Branca, Bourbon, and Carpano Antica Glaze for Pork Shoulder

This is one of the best, and easiest, ways to cook pork shoulder that I can imagine. Bourbon, Carpano Antica—that's Italian sweet vermouth—and Fernet Branca make a magnificent marinade in which your pork and vegetables are steeped before being popped in the oven for the afternoon. Go ahead and use an inexpensive cut of pork shoulder: Long, slow cooking means that the meat will be melt-in-your-mouth tender. And the best part is, after the first half hour of cooking, you can leave the dish in the oven and forget about it for six hours. It'll smell divine, but whatever you do, don't open the lid until the thing is out of the oven and has "rested" on the counter for a while—opening the lid too soon ruins the dish.

---

1 (5 pounds, or 2.25 kg) **pork shoulder (fatty cuts work best and taste amazing!)**

2 tablespoons (30 ml) **Fernet Branca**

½ cup (15 ml) **Carpano Antica**

1 bulb garlic: **slice off the top ⅓ of the bulb, but leave the papery skin on**

½ cup (65 g) **chopped carrot**

½ cup (50 g) **chopped celery**

½ cup (55 g) **chopped parsnip**

¼ cup (7 ml) **bourbon**

1 chopped **onion**

1 bunch **fresh sage**

1 sprig **rosemary**

1 bunch **thyme**

....

*Combine the bourbon, Carpano Antica, and Fernet Branca. Place the pork shoulder, the vegetables, and the herbs in a Dutch oven, and pour the liquor over them. Leave in the refrigerator overnight to marinate. The next day, preheat the oven to 400°F (200°C, or gas mark 6), and add 1 to 2 cups (235 to 475 ml) of spring water to the mixture. Place the Dutch oven in the oven and roast for 30 minutes at 400°F (200°C, or gas mark 6), and then drop the temperature down to 250°F (120°C, or gas mark ½). Cook for about 6 hours. (It's almost impossible to cook this dish for **too** long!) Serve with a rye whiskey–laden Late Summer Fizz (see page 102): Its appley crispness is perfect with pork.*

Hearty Barley, Lentil, and Vegetable Stew

Naturally vegan and wheat-free, my Hearty Barley, Lentil, and Vegetable Stew is proof that cooking with whiskey doesn't necessarily mean cooking with meat. And I guarantee you won't miss the meat in this stick-to-your-ribs stew. Easily made with stuff you probably already have on hand in the kitchen, it's both healthy and substantial—and it'll fill your house with the most amazing aroma. It's great in winter weather, but to be honest, I make it year-round. Just before serving, I like to add a 2-ounce (60-ml) whack of Scotch to the bowl for a little extra warming—but feel free to substitute bourbon, if that's your poison. Serve with a hunk of fresh, crusty bread, or half a baguette, since you'll want to soak up every last drop of Scotch and stew alike.

½ cup (100 g) **dried pearl barley** ½ cup (96 g) **dried red lentils**

½ cup (112 g) **dried split peas** About 4 quarts (3.8 L) **vegetable stock**

Olive oil

Freshly ground black pepper **Sea salt**

2 **Spanish onions, finely diced** 3 to 4 finely diced **shallots**

2 **carrots, finely diced** 2 finely diced **turnips**

3 **stalks celery, finely diced** 2 finely chopped **all-purpose potatoes**

1 **leek, washed three times, trimmed, and roughly chopped**

6 **whole cloves of garlic, smashed with the side of your knife**

3 tablespoons (9 g) each **roughly chopped Italian parsley & celery leaves**

2 ounces (60 ml) **per serving smoky Scotch whisky, or bourbon**

Cover the dried pulses in 2 quarts (1.9 L) of the vegetable stock and soak overnight. The next day, preheat your oven to 300°F (150°C, or gas mark 2). In a large vessel like a cast-iron Dutch oven, sauté the onions, carrots, turnips, celery, potatoes, and leek in olive oil until soft and nicely browned. Add the barley, lentils, split peas, shallots, garlic, parsley, and celery leaves to the sautéing vegetables, and stir to combine. Add the remaining vegetable stock. Place the Dutch oven into the oven, and bake for 1 to 2 hours, occasionally adding enough stock to give the stew a thick consistency instead of a thinner, soupy one. You may have stock left over. Season to taste before serving. Serve in preheated ceramic bowls, and pour the Scotch or bourbon whisky over the top of each bowl just before serving. For a little extra healing warmth, serve with a Sailor's Dilemma, a simple combination of beef broth and Scotch whisky (see page 122).

Oatmeal Raisin Whoopie Pies

Drambuie is a Scotch-whisky-based liqueur that smacks of sea salt, honey, and herbs, and it adds an unmistakably grown-up quality to these homemade whoopie pies. Mix up a batch of these easy-to-make oatmeal raisin cookies—featuring Drambuie-laced raisins, of course—and slather them with the rich cream cheese filling for a dreamy finish to dinnertime.

For the cookies:

1 cup (145 g) **raisins**   1 cup (235 ml) **Drambuie**

2 sticks **unsalted butter at room temperature**

1 cup (225 g) **light brown sugar, well packed**

1 large **egg at room temperature**   1 tablespoon (15 ml) **vanilla**

⅓ cup (78 ml) **maple syrup**   1½ cups (192 g) **unbleached flour**

½ cup (42 g) **sweetened, desiccated coconut**

½ teaspoon **kosher salt**   1 teaspoon (5 g) **cinnamon**

1 teaspoon (5 g) **ground ginger**   1 teaspoon (5 g) **baking soda**

3 cups (240 g) **steel-cut oats (not the "instant" variety!)**

For the filling:

1 (8 ounces or 227 g) package of **cream cheese**

3 cups (360 g) **sifted confectioner's sugar**

1 teaspoon (5 ml) **vanilla**   ¼ cup (60 ml) **maple syrup**

Preheat the oven to 350°F (180°C, or gas mark 4), and line 2 baking sheets with parchment paper in a saucepan, cover raisins with the Drambuie and place over a low flame. Let simmer for 5 minutes or until the liquid is almost gone. Drain off the liquid and discard (it'll taste bitter), and set aside the raisins to cool. Using a handheld mixer set on low, cream the butter and sugar in a large bowl. Add the egg, vanilla, and maple syrup, and continue to beat on low. Then add the flour, coconut, salt, cinnamon, ginger, and baking soda until just combined. Finally, add the oats and raisins. Using a 2-inch (5-cm) scoop, place the cookies about 2 inches (5 cm) apart on the tray. Bake in the center of the oven for about 15 minutes. Let cool on a wire rack. Yields about 24 cookies. To make the filling, simply combine all ingredients in a large bowl, and, using a stand mixer, beat until smooth and creamy. To make the whoopie pies, spread a tablespoon (15 g) or two of the filling onto a cookie, and then top with another to form a sandwich. Makes 12 whoopie pies. Wash them down with a General Jack's Crisp Apple Fizz (see page 43).

SYRUPS, INFUSIONS, AND LOTS MORE

Basic Simple Syrup. In a medium saucepan, combine 1 cup (235 ml) of water and 1 cup (200 g) of bar sugar or caster sugar and bring to a boil, mixing until the sugar has dissolved. Let the mixture cool. Keep refrigerated in an airtight container for up to a month.

The Best Hot Chocolate. Mix ½ cup (100 g) of the best-quality bittersweet chocolate powder (ideally, seventy-five percent cocoa) with 1 cup (235 ml) whole milk and ½ cup (115 g) heavy cream. Over a low heat, slowly whisk the mixture until it reaches a smooth consistency, and sweeten to taste with Basic Simple Syrup. Finish with a pinch of freshly grated nutmeg.

Curried Bitters. Simply add 1 teaspoon (5 g) of curry powder to 3 tablespoons (45 g) of Angostura Bitters and mix well. Refrigerate and store indefinitely.

Easy Home-Cured Cocktail Cherries. Pit a pound of black cherries, and place in a non-reactive bowl or jar and cover. Cover them with bourbon or Scotch whiskey, and place the bowl in the fridge to steep for a couple weeks. Use in cocktails, non-alcoholic drinks, on ice cream, or even in oatmeal!

Frozen Hot Chocolate. Prepare a serving of The Best Hot Chocolate. Pour into an ice cube tray, and freeze for 8 hours or overnight. Then put the ice cubes into a plastic food-storage bag or a Lewis bag, and, using a wooden rolling pin, crush into pebbles.

Ginger Honey Simple Syrup. Make a batch of Raw Honey Simple Syrup. Add ¼ cup (25 g) finely chopped fresh (preferably young) ginger. Pour the mixture into an airtight container, and let it steep in the fridge for a couple days. Strain before using. Use within 2 weeks.

Grilled Citrus Juices. To make 1 cup (235 ml) of each citrus juice:

Orange: Cut 2 to 3 oranges into ½-inch (1.25-cm) thick slices. Place the slices on a grill or grill pan, and cook until char marks appear on the flesh of the fruit.

Grapefruit: Cut 1 to 2 grapefruits into ½-inch (1.25-cm) thick slices. Place the slices on a grill or grill pan, and cook until char marks appear on the flesh of the fruit.

Pineapple: Slice 1 pineapple into wedges ½-inch (1.25-cm) thick, removing the rind. Place the slices on a grill or grill pan, and cook until char marks appear on the flesh of the fruit.

To juice: Remove any peel or rind that may remain on the fruit. Cut into pieces small enough to fit into a juicer, and put them one at a time into the juicer. Strain the juices before using. Store them in airtight containers for up to 1 week.

Homemade Grenadine Syrup. Combine 2 ounces (60 ml) Basic Simple Syrup, 2 cups (475 ml) pomegranate juice, and ¼ teaspoon each nutmeg, cinnamon, and cayenne pepper in a medium saucepan. Bring to a simmer, then reduce the heat and continue to simmer for 15 to 20 minutes. Allow the mixture to cool, and then use a funnel to transfer it to a glass bottle. Add no more than four drops of orange water—and, if you like, some overproof rum or vodka for extra zip.

Homemade Whipped Cream. Combine 1 pint (473 ml) of heavy whipping cream with 2 tablespoons (26 g) of confectioner's sugar. (To make **Coffee Whipped Cream**, add 1 tablespoon (13 g) of powdered espresso coffee. To make **Cognac Whipped Cream**, add a few drops of cognac.) Whip with a whisk until the mixture reaches a softly creamy, almost pourable, consistency. (You don't want to make butter, so don't over-whisk the cream!)

Luscious Asian Fruit Puree. Peel and deseed 1 orange, 1 jackfruit, 1 Asian pear, and 1 starfruit. Puree in a food processor, and then press through a fine sieve to remove any remaining skin or seeds. Store in an airtight container in the refrigerator for up to a week.

Orange Simple Syrup. In a medium saucepan, combine 1 cup (20 g) sugar, ½ cup (120 ml) freshly squeezed orange juice (strained), and 2 tablespoons (12 g) grated orange zest, and ½ cup (120 ml) water. Simmer, mixing until the sugar has dissolved. Let the mixture cool. Strain before using, and keep refrigerated in an airtight container for up to 2 weeks.

Quince Puree. Preheat your oven to 250°F (120°C, or gas mark ½). Cut 1 quince into ½-inch (1.25-cm) chunks, and place on a baking tray. (Be careful when slicing the quince: It's rock-hard, and your knife can slip easily, leading to nasty kitchen accidents! Be sure to secure your cutting board first by placing a wet dish towel underneath it.) Roast the quince for at least 4 hours, until soft. When cool, put the quince into a food mill in order to remove the skin and the bitter pits. Reserve as much of the liquid as possible. Refrigerate in an airtight container for up to 1 week.

Raw Honey Simple Syrup. In a medium saucepan, combine 1 cup (340 g) honey with ½ cup (120 ml) water and simmer, mixing until the honey has dissolved. Let the mixture cool. Keep refrigerated in an airtight container for up to a month.

Roasted Stone Fruits. Line a baking tray with parchment paper, and preheat your oven to 300°F (150°C, or gas mark 2). Slice 1 pound (455 g) assorted stone fruits, such as peaches, plums, and/or apricots, in half (pits removed). Sprinkle with demerara sugar, and roast slowly for 3 hours. Let the stone fruits cool overnight in as much of their own liquid as possible. Drizzle Raw Honey Simple Syrup over them to keep moist. Store in an airtight container in the refrigerator for up to a week (any longer and they tend to get fuzzy!).

Roasted Strawberries. Preheat your oven to 300°F (150°C, or gas mark 2). Stem about a pound of strawberries, and place them in a cast-iron frying pan. Roast for about 1 hour, or until melted and soft. Let cool. Refrigerate in an airtight container for up to 1 week.

Rosemary Simple Syrup. Make a batch of Basic Simple Syrup. Crumble a handful of rosemary leaves, place them in a cheesecloth bag, and submerge the bag in the Basic Simple Syrup. Let the mixture cool. Remove the cheesecloth bag, pour the mixture into an airtight container, and store in the fridge for up to 1 month.

Spicy Ginger Honey Simple Syrup. Make a batch of Raw Ginger Honey Simple Syrup, and add ½ teaspoon cayenne pepper. Pour the mixture into an airtight container, and let it steep in the fridge for a couple days. Strain before using. Use within 2 weeks.

Spicy Simple Syrup. In a medium saucepan, combine 2 cups (400 g) of sugar with 1 cup (235 ml) of water and bring to a boil, mixing until the sugar has dissolved. Let the mixture cool. Add a tablespoon of chopped poblano and/or ancho chiles. Pour the mixture into an airtight container, and let it steep in the fridge for a couple days. Strain before using. Use within 2 weeks.

Vietnamese Fizzy Lemonade. Chop 2 to 3 preserved lemons (available in Asian supermarkets). Add them to a pitcher, combine with 4 tablespoons (52 g) of sugar, a ¼ teaspoon sea salt, and top with fizzy water to taste.

Acknowledgments

I'd like to acknowledge my friends in the independent spirits world who have filled my soul with potent consumables.

I'll acknowledge those who encourage me to taste, and not necessarily to drink, but also to dream and to follow my dreams.

To Tales of the Cocktail, The Manhattan Cocktail Classic, and the Indie Sprits gatherings in New Orleans, Chicago and New York for guiding me to new flavors and brands outside of the big players in our industry.

I've done my best to follow my ambition when most around me wanted me to fail so they could say "I told you that you should have been an accountant."

I didn't fail. No accountant here.

Whiskey Cocktails has taken me past the expected and into the unexpected. I tasted things and continue to expand my palate into places I never thought possible. *Whiskey Cocktails* taught me to be knowledgeable yet humble, a go to for ideas, yet I'm learning in each and every sip.

To the magazines, encyclopedias, and blogs who include me in the fun and help me continue to do what I love.

For this I say, thank you.

About the Author

Warren Bobrow is the food and drink editor of Wild River Review, in Princeton, New Jersey. He was one of twelve journalists worldwide, and the only one from the United States, to participate in the Fête de la Gastronomie, held September 2012, in the Burgundy region of France. He attends Tales of the Cocktail and The Manhattan Cocktail Classic yearly. Warren is the former owner and cofounder of Olde Charleston Pasta in Charleston, South Carolina, while cooking at the Primerose House and Tavern (also in Charleston). He has published over 300 articles on everything from cocktail mixology to restaurant reviews to travel articles. Warren was #30 in *Saveur* magazine's 100 in 2010 for his writing about the humble tuna melt. He also writes for the "Fabulous Beekman 1802 Boys" as their cocktail writer (Klaus, the Soused Gnome).

You may find Warren on the web at www.cocktailwhisperer.com

Index

159